FRANKLIN D ISRAEL

To Dean Blocker

my second book to a testimony
to my students influence on me,
Their input and enthusiasm.

I am looking forward to discussing it and
the work with you

best.

Frank 1994.

Architectural Monographs No 34

FRANKLIN D ISRAEL

A.D. ACADEMY EDITIONS

Acknowledgements

I dedicate this book to Barbara Callas, Annie Chu, and Steven Shortridge.
The works included in this book are a testament to their creative energy,
and bear witness to their uncompromising commitment to architecture. I
salute them and thank them deeply.
I would like to acknowledge the assistance of the following persons in
preparing the drawings and other documents in this book. Staff: Felix Ang,
Fernando Bracer, Jay Deguchi, Rick Gooding, Joseph Holsen, Danny
Kaplan, Austin Kelly, Christian Lynch, Michael Matteucci, William Molthen,
Scott Oliver, Scott Parker, Carol Patterson, Thomas Rael, Sean Reardon,
Elaine René-Weissman, Seth Rosenthal, Lindy Roy, Jefferson Schierbeek,
Tomas Schuler, Leslie Shapiro, Rocky Shen, Steve Sheng, James Simeo,
Mark Tholen, Jim Chang Tsai, Sandra Ventura, Elizabeth Villaba, Michael
Volk, Keith Wilen, George Yu, Tom Zook. Princeton exhibit coordination
and assistance: Alastair Gordon, Mehmet Dogu, Lori Brown, John Cays,
Natalie Fizer, Lisa Neely, Noel Williams. I would like to thank Joe Day and
especially Terry Bissel for helping me to edit the text of the interview.
Special gratitude also goes to Kamal Kozah for his great support and
creative advice.

Franklin D Israel

Photograpic credits
Baldwin Tom Bonner; *Belldegrun* Art Gray; *Drager* Tom Bonner; *Jupiter*
Tom Bonner; *Goldberg-Bean* David Glomb pp45 below, 46 below, 49
below; Jenny Okun pp53, 54-5 above; Tom Bonner (all others); *Hague I*
Tom Bonner (model); Michael Moran (titanium box); *Spartan* Art Gray; *Woo
Fong* Jenny Okun pp72-3, 76-7; Grant Mudford (all others); *Bright and
Associates* Mark Darley/Esto Photographics pp78, 84, 84-5, 86-7, 89),
Robert Markovitch pp80-1, 90, 91, Grant Mudford pp79, 81, 89, 90-1, 92,
93; *Bunka Shutter* Tom Bonner; *Limelight* Grant Mudford (interiors); Tom
Bonner (exterior); *Prompt* Arch Photo/Eduard Hueber; *UCLA-SRL* Jock
Pottle; *Virgin* Tom Bonner (model); Robert Markovich pp123, 124-5, 130-1,
136-7; Grant Mudford (all others); *Strick* Grant Mudford.

Cover: Virgin Records, exterior; *Page 2:* Bright and Associates, interior.
(Photographs by Robert Markovich.)

House Editor: Maggie Toy
Art Editor: Andrea Bettella
Designers: Jacqueline Grosvenor, Jan Richter
Senior Editor: Iona Spens
Editor: Pamela Johnston

First published in Great Britain in 1994 by
ACADEMY EDITIONS
An imprint of the Academy Group Ltd
Editorial Offices
42 Leinster Gardens London W2 3AN
Member of VCH Publishing Group

ISBN 1 85490 274 1 (PB)

Distributed in the United States of America in 1994 by
ST MARTIN'S PRESS
175 Fifth Avenue, New York, NY 10012

Printed and bound in Singapore

CONTENTS

FOREWORD

Los Angeles is unique. This city was designed to allow people to avoid one another, and it is very successful in that respect.

With both irony and realism I have been pursuing the peculiarly isolating architectures of southern California for almost two decades now. After training in Philadelphia and New York, and travelling extensively through Europe and Asia, I arrived in Los Angeles in 1977 eager to reach a synthesis between my architectural education and the cinematic intrigues of Hollywood. Though my list of commissions reflects an early fixation with filmmaking, my architecture has developed into a collection of urban engagements as concerned with the subtle art of city-building as inspired by the products and personalities of 'The Industry'.

Like one of my earliest clients, the director Robert Altman, I see Los Angeles as an episodic collage, woven together more by the demands of nature than by the concerted forces of political clout and economic necessity that structure traditional cities. The diffuse tragedy and poetry of such a city are realised at ground level, where tyres leave their marks, and echoed in the low sprawl of the entire landscape. My buildings seek to expose these exigencies, revealing the tensions of an architecture engaged with an unstable earth and an even less predictable urban environment. The most recent work in my office revels in the competing impulses to both secure against and pay homage to these powerful forces. Building on the tradition of Californian modernism, it couples the topographical and ecological sensitivities of Rudolph Schindler with the expressive freedoms and guarded urbanity of my more immediate mentor, Frank Gehry.

When not mistaken for the perennial city of the future, Los Angeles is all too often misunderstood in relation to its past. Futurism and nostalgia are the poles by which many of her architects orient their careers. I have abandoned this model, opting, like Schindler, for the immediacy of site and circumstance. Mine is not an ideal, eternal present, but a reality of building shared by office, clients and an often intractable city.

A man's home in Los Angeles may or may not be his castle, but it will almost certainly be as well secured as one. To accept this condition is to face the threat that such introversion poses to urban interaction. Public space is residual in Los Angeles, but most designers here refuse to acknowledge this, calling instead for variations of Old World urbanism. These schemes fail to account for the pace of life in the city and the degree to which that pace depends on both the isolation and the freedom of the automobile. From fortified private homes and gated communities to closed office parks and thematic, semi-private shopping centres, security concerns have curtailed public interaction. However, when one slips out of the 'designed' urban fabric, one stumbles immediately into thousands of incidental situations. Once the bane of urbanists, the lowly corner mall has become Los Angeles' most enduring hope for civic space; it represents as central and complex a design issue as the piazza did in fifteenth-century Italy.

In this sense, the city designed to allow people to avoid one another need not be read pessimistically. A mixed feat of social, ecological and structural engineering, Los Angeles is a place where, although dreams are realised in private, they *are* realised, and at a scale of personal expression possible almost nowhere else. Monitoring the ebb and flow of a city built on foundations of sand, I attempt in this work to reinterpret the landscape of LA in light of its transience. *Frank Israel*

OPPOSITE: Limelight Productions

▌NTRODUCTION

In a city in which anything that happened yesterday is considered to be passé, a recognition of and allegiance to historical influence by any architect goes beyond eccentricity to become an act of sheer courage. For Frank Israel, that recognition is wide ranging, exceeding even the rich typologies of Los Angeles. This higher perspective allows him to identify connections at various degrees of magnification, and to demonstrate to those who distrust the past that, rather than being a restrictive liability, precedent can be a liberating gift, providing the possibility for greater originality.

Like a majority of others in Los Angeles, Frank Israel was not born there. He came to his adopted city from New York, after having already gained the considerable experience as an architect and planner that has contributed to his understanding of the complexities of the urban condition. Travel, especially to Rome, has extended that knowledge, further allowing him to identify layers, patterns and complexities that have consistently eluded others.

In making a comparison between Los Angeles and Rome at the height of its power, Israel has coined the term 'dialogical' to describe the way that both cities have derived legitimacy from external sources, possessing no stable internal basis on which to construct it. His latest work confirms this comparison by reinforcing and amplifying such external, legitimising connections, as well as newer, local ones, to give a refreshingly objective view of the contemporary condition. He shares, with his acknowledged mentor Frank Gehry, a desire to create idealised communities in a city in which vast distances, fragmentation and an unpredictable, elemental environment conspire to defeat less informed attempts to achieve human scale of the kind usually associated with the East Coast of the United States. Now that Los Angeles has finally usurped the position of New York (its undeclared civic *alter ego*) as the main immigration gateway into America, the character of such miniaturised urban enclaves, as interpreted by Israel, has changed to eloquently articulated defensible 'cities within'.

Israel's reconstructions are not like the abstracted conurbations created by Gehry: the microcosmic mill town in Brentwood, or the reinterpretation of the Parthenon on Pico. His pavilions, regardless of scale, relate to a different frame of reference, with an individualised choice of symbols and materials to match. As Gehry has said: 'Frank and I have a lot of common ground. Both of us absorb our surroundings, recast what we see, and examine how these realities impact on the human psyche.' That recasting revolves around a personal vision which is manifested in the whole, the unusual treatment of space, form, contour and colour; and in the intricate detailing of the emergant architecture.

The architecture of Frank Israel responds with a sensitivity that effectively separates him from other highly publicised architects in Los Angeles. However, his most distinguishing characteristic of all is his humanity – his widely acknowledged ability to empathise with those who actually use the buildings he has created. It is this, undoubtedly, which will ensure that Israel continues to make a significant contribution in an effervescent city best known for its temporality.   *James Steele*

OPPOSITE: Bright and Associates

James Steele and Franklin D Israel

NTERVIEW

James Steele: My first question is, I guess, the one everyone begins with. What is your background here? Did you begin with the entertainment industry, or with something else entirely?

Frank Israel: I actually came to California to teach architecture.

JS: Where?

FI: At UCLA. I was hired by Charles Moore, whom I knew from Yale University and later the American Academy in Rome. After about four years in Europe I had returned to New York City and was working for Jaquelin Robertson on the Museum of Modern Art Tower project that he was designing with Cesar Pelli.

JS: What year was this?

FI: It was 1976. I had enjoyed Europe immensely and I wasn't particularly happy to be back in New York. The architectural community had become quite incestuous. It was a club of which you were either a member or not. The project for the Museum of Modern Art Tower was fascinating, but it had a lot of problems. When I had completed my work on it, I got a phone call from Charles Moore, asking if I would be willing to come to UCLA to teach for ten weeks as a visiting studio critic. Two weeks after I arrived, one of my students mentioned that her husband, who was in the film industry, was looking for someone to do drafting. I needed to make some extra money because the teaching was only part-time, so I took a job with Bob Abel. Bob was a fascinating guy. He liked architecture, and was building a house in Santa Monica Canyon designed by Charles Moore. He had studied for a while with Charles and Ray Eames and his company, Robert Abel Films, was loaded

with some of the most talented people in the city. He hired me to work on the first 'Star Trek' motion picture, for which he was designing all the special effects. It was a remarkable opportunity; it gave me the chance to get exposed to the film industry. After finishing my work with Abel, I moved to the Philippines for six months and worked on a couple of movies there. One was by Roger Vadim, the other was by Raymond Chow, the Chinese film producer. When I got back to Los Angeles, I returned to UCLA to teach and continued to dabble in the film industry, working on a few Roger Corman movies and putting together ideas for a series of other film and video projects.

Eventually, I shelved my interest in the entertainment industry. I realised there were a few things about movies that didn't appeal to me and that I felt uncomfortable with. One is that the product is ultimately a piece of celluloid. No matter how well you design something, if it's not photographed well, it's not going to look good. I found myself becoming increasingly frustrated because my sets and special effects were being shot by cinematographers who were more interested in sparkles and flares than they were in representing a set correctly. Some of the film projects I worked on were shot entirely in close-up, so that you couldn't see the sets at all. The other problem was that the film industry lacked the sense of tradition that I had always cherished in architecture. I realised that I couldn't really juggle the two. So I made the decision to concentrate on architecture – to continue to teach and to open a design office. The time I spent at Bob Abel's and Paramount served me well in the end because I made a lot of good contacts. I was always presented to people as an architect who was working in the film industry. My clients turned out to be directors and producers and cinematographers who were becoming increasingly successful. They bought houses that needed to be fixed up, or opened their own film studios with offices that had to be planned and designed. The latter turned out to be some of my most important commissions.

JS: Has your exposure to clients in the entertainment industry – to their sort of world view, their personas and their life styles – directed you in the way that you design?

FI: It has, certainly. For example, the Virgin Records and Pittard Sullivan Fitzgerald projects that we are presently working on are based on an interest in cinematography and an understanding of how a film evolves through storyboards, from which drawn scenes are shot on film. Sequential reality is essential in developing a story; these projects use a similar method of sequence procession in their planning and realisation. I learned, when I did my first big studio design for Propaganda Films, that a studio is organised in almost the same way a film is. There is a beginning, middle, and end. At Bright and Associates, for example, the entry lobby is pulled into the office wing by a steel-clad tunnel. Progressing from there, the sequence of the spaces terminates with a sculptural tower made of steel and stacked glass.

JS: Another connection comes to mind. Robert Venturi was, like you, a Fellow at the American Academy in Rome, and you followed his classes at Philadelphia. Are there any parallels between your work and that of the Philadelphia School?

FI: Yes. My exposure to both Venturi and Kahn in those years had a profound effect on my development. When I arrived in 1963, Kahn was teaching at the University of Pennsylvania and Venturi was building the house for his mother. The city was creatively rich and active. David Crane was working there, so were Ian McHarg, Robert Le Ricolais, Romaldo Giurgola, Robert Geddes, Richard Saul Wurman and others. It was a very exciting time; the motor behind it all was Louis Kahn. There was Kahn the teacher and Kahn the catalyst, generating a tremendous amount of creative activity. Of course, Venturi owes a lot to Kahn. Some people say his work was influenced by Alvar Aalto, among others. But I don't think he would have become as important if it hadn't been for Kahn. When I first saw Venturi's work, I found it utterly obtuse. But at the same time I was drawn to it: I felt there was something extraordinary about it, something I needed to understand better. I was able to understand it by hanging around Bob in his studio, by

following his classes, and, of course, by reading his book. When I read *Complexity and Contradiction in Architecture*, I realised that I wanted to study with Bob more directly, so I left Pennsylvania and went to Yale, where he was doing the Las Vegas studios. It was a very exciting time to be there.

The Philadelphia School evolved by fashioning ideas in formal arrangements that celebrated urban life. Most of the significant built works were either single-family houses or infill projects. In this respect, the Philadelphia School in the 1960s has a distinct relationship to that of LA in the 1980s. But the architecture of LA today, stylistically speaking, is completely different from what prevailed in Philadelphia in the 1960s. Ironically, many of the people who helped to define the Philadelphia School have moved west. Tim Vreeland, Jack MacAllister and David Rinehart, who worked on the Salk Institute in La Jolla, chose to remain in California and open their own offices. Barton Myers and Richard Weinstein, who were students of Kahn's, came here to work and to teach at UCLA. The work of these men is rooted in their past: it is formalist and tight compared to that of the LA School.

Frank Gehry was also instrumental in drawing me to Los Angeles. When I first looked at LA, I saw an abrasive and ugly place. But as I studied Gehry's architecture and his reactions to the city, I became more and more mesmerised. The ad hoc nature of his work reflects LA's own disconnection and lack of harmony. Gehry opened my eyes to the city's aesthetics; from looking around I grew to understand what was special about it. He helped me see this world for what it is: a richly diverse environment representative of the demographics and plurality of these times. Like Kahn in Philadelphia, Gehry set the platform for a younger generation of architects to work and flourish here. Moss, Morphosis, Hodgetts and myself owe much to Frank: he is a pioneer who forged a path in what was once a barren wilderness. But while my work owes much to Gehry, it also reflects many of the details and methods of construction developed by Charles and Ray Eames. In Gehry's work collisions occur in which materials and forms are juxtaposed. My projects define joints and, as with the work of the Eameses, these expressions of linkages become the point of the architecture. This is certainly true of the Goldberg-Bean house and Bright and Associates, which was built from the original Eames offices.

JS: You've raised two important issues which I think can help to get to the heart of what you're doing: namely, historicism and urbanism. I was in Philadelphia probably around the same time as you, and my experience was that Kahn and Venturi were the first ones to really break down the modernist barriers against historicism, to look at the past as something worthy of study. Also, because you've lived on the East Coast and in Europe, you have a sense of the tradition of urbanism that's missing in LA. Some people would say that LA has no history at all, which is ridiculous. Its history is just shorter than that of the East Coast. If you look at Gehry's work, you'll see that it's not based on the same kind of historical models. He had no tradition like Kahn or Venturi to follow, although you may find, in his buildings, references to Wright and to other people.

FI: Loyola Law School, a project Gehry was first designing when I moved here, represents his one foray into classicism. A series of classroom pavilions sit in front of a long horizontal administration/library building. The relationship is spelt out: the pavilions are object pieces set against a hard-edged backdrop. Gehry chose to upset the order by inserting a colossal stair into his scheme that becomes the major circulation element. The stair twists itself up and down and through this block; it is both a figural and functional element in the design. He used a similar strategy with the Yale Psychiatric Institute in New Haven. Both of these projects represent another theme prevalent in Los Angeles today: the city as a series of separate sanctuaries. Certainly, Loyola, with its walls and fences, does not invite people in – rather it pulls them apart and defends them.

I think it's revealing to look at the relationship we all have to the case study architects who worked in LA in the 1950s – Eames and Pierre Koenig and others whose buildings evoke a period of great optimism in the city. The work that we see now in LA reflects the pessimism of the moment. Life here has changed radically in the last fifteen years. This used to be a place where you could leave your front door open. You don't do that anymore. To quote a friend of mine, this is a city where you're no longer safe anywhere you are. As a result, the architecture we are building is defensible. It sends out a message: 'Keep out. Stay away.' The work in Philadelphia was also very much about walls, but there they served to define an inner realm rather than protect a space**.**

JS: You've heard, no doubt, of *Cities Within*. Do you think that this is a self-fulfilling kind of prophecy, that architecture has become more introspective as people themselves have become more introspective?

FI: Not necessarily. Los Angeles has always been a city comprised of separate towns and villages. The film studios, and more recently, the theme parks and shopping malls, have reinforced this character. Famous people enjoy living here because the city encourages its inhabitants to build walls and isolate themselves in their own domains.

JS: It seems to me the issue of security is critical. Whereas in the past such architects as Wright or Eames or Neutra would connect with the site, now, because of security, the environment is no longer considered a primary element. But in your work there seems to be an additional layer of relating to the site. Is this something you deliberately try to do?

FI: Personally, I have always felt that the most important thing about any project is the site. It is the site that generates the ideas. One person whom I respect and have learned much from is Rudolph Schindler. I find his work extraordinarily rich: it's loaded with notions about the site. We used his Wolfe House on Catalina Island, which steps very dramatically downhill, as a model for the Drager House in Berkeley. And the project we're doing in Florida, the Jupiter House, is very similar to Schindler's Kings Road House. Both sit on flat sites and segregate themselves from the street. Our house also sits on the inner coastal waterway; the landscaping creates a series of defined spaces that relate directly to what's happening inside. Schindler was an extremely original architect. He never executed any public architecture, though he was much more inventive than Neutra, who had outstanding commissions.

Perhaps Schindler would not have been so experimental if he had had bigger budgets. His clients were willing to take risks. We've always enjoyed working on projects that are not too expensive because those clients are similarly open to taking risks.

I had my office in Schindler's house on Kings Road for a couple of years and had a chance to experience it during periods when it was hot and cold, wet and dry. I discovered from living in his work that it truly integrates itself into its setting. You rarely come across anything like it on the East Coast – though one exception I saw recently was a Neutra house in Philadelphia where he had carved out the site and done something very beautiful with it.

I think the relationship between landscape and architecture is much more defined here than on the East Coast. My explanation for this is our proximity to the Pacific Rim. Asian art, and certainly the architecture of Japan, has been a source of inspiration for many

of us who have come to California to live and work.

JS: The Japanese connection is interesting because their architecture has to do with motion, with the relationship between outside and inside, which brings us back again to the security issue, to defensible architecture.

FI: Today we are encouraged to build castles. However, on the West Coast, building and landscape are unified into a harmonious whole in which security plays an important part.

JS: Where do you think your work is going now? You're getting bigger commissions all the time.

FI: We've just started work on an arts facility for the University of California at Riverside. It's a 120,000-square-foot building on a beautiful site, at the edge of an arroyo. I'm very excited about it because it's going to give us the opportunity to play with different ideas about the relationship of building to landscape and the dialogue that exists between the inside and the outside. The nature of this site is inspiring us to design outdoor spaces that are sculpted into it.

To describe the direction of the office in more general terms, I'm going to quote Dagmar Richter, who was here recently. She took a look at some of our projects and said, 'Gee, you're really involved in folded planes.' You can see this happening in our first house at The Hague, the Drager House, the Jupiter House and the Venice headquarters of Pittard Sullivan and Fitzgerald.

JS: Can you explain this more?

FI: Folding a facade back so that it becomes the roof is one way of relating plan to elevation. It also provides us with a way of enclosing space in which vertical and horizontal components are united. At the Drager House, the folded planes of the roof and front and side elevations help to integrate the building into its setting. Here the building steps up the site, and the bending of the facade into the roof pulls the house into a complex and unfragmented whole.

JS: There are intriguing theoretical parallels to this, because some people are now trying to follow ideas about folding related to mathematics.

FI: Folding strategies have arisen out of a variety of concerns – mathematics and physics, for some; conceptual and minimalist art practices for others. My interest in folding has mostly to do with the intersection of architecture and landscape, with the implications of removing, replacing and reorienting the ground plane. A flat roof sets up a planar relationship with the ground. When it is combined with a folded plane, it can create an extremely exciting and energising set of relationships, especially when the facade and roof are the same.

JS: With your emphasis on roofs, you are returning to the basic idea of shelter. This makes your work very different from those exponents of folding who are talking about decentring, about moving architecture away from human use. It seems to me that human beings are very much a part of your architecture.

FI: Our clients generate many of our ideas. The house we did for Michael Woo and Susan Fong in Silver Lake, for example, grew out of a very strict programme. We first added a series of bedrooms to the house because they wanted to enlarge their family. But they also wanted to have something that was very much for the two of them – a place to hang out, a place to sleep, a place for them to engage with the site. Until we built this addition, they didn't have a view of the lake, and they had no sense of the nature of the hillside that is behind their property. What we did was create a building that climbs up to a loft area, conceived as a retreat for the two of them, with a studio and a master bedroom looking out towards Silver Lake.

There are two things going on here. One is the celebration of the hillside to the rear, with the stairs stepping up at the same grade, and the other is a room at the top of the house, with its beautiful views of the lake. Silver Lake's a wonderful place in this city. It is filled with houses by Neutra and Schindler, and it has always attracted some of the most interesting and creative people.

JS: Looking at the city in general now, many people are disturbed by the direction it's taking. Do you think that architects operating at your level can have any kind of impact on the situation? Can they change it for the better?

FI: I don't think there is very much we can do in LA. Things here are quite different from Philadelphia, where the dean of the School of Architecture at Penn, G Holmes Perkins, was also head of the city planning commission. Along with Ed Bacon, he was engaged in manipulating a political institution in order to promote a particular kind of architecture and urban vision for the future. On the other hand, Los Angeles architects like myself and Thom Mayne and Eric Moss tend to be detached from politics. Things may change. We have a mayor right now who says he's interested in promoting architecture for the city, and his relationship with Frank Gehry may have some very positive repercussions, though it's a little too early to say. In general, LA is an apolitical place. If you walked around the city and asked people what the name of the mayor was, you'd find out that half of them didn't know. In Philadelphia and New York, that's not the case. They know. They are engaged. This city is about being disengaged.

JS: What chance does the strategic plan for downtown LA have to succeed?

FI: The plan for downtown LA is not well integrated into the character and nature of the city. It's absurd – and they've put too much money into it. I think Hollywood should have been given a much bigger push. LA is not a city focused on a downtown. It has a number of nuclei, all with very different characters. As architects, we should be reinforcing the characters of these different places. This doesn't mean that downtown can't be important and exciting, although I doubt that it's going to be. I don't think that the cultural institutions there are going to attract a lot of people. And I don't think people will use the subway, either. They'll still get into their cars and drive downtown, park in a garage, go to an event and then drive back to Santa Monica or Encino.

JS: So it's going to be more of the same thing?

FI: I just don't see people going downtown to hang out. And that's OK with me. I personally don't like downtown LA. A few years ago everyone was moving downtown into lofts, but I couldn't see the point. It's not like New York, where there's an incredible street life. In SoHo, you run into people you know on the street. You have artists living on top of other artists. You have galleries, great restaurants, wonderful shops . . . a whole kind of existence that downtown LA is never going to have because of the automobile. When I was in Philadelphia, I was very much against the automobile: I saw what it had done to American cities. Now, whenever I go anywhere, I have to have a car. Not having one is frustrating. In New

York and Chicago it's cool just to run out and get a taxi. But there's something about having one's own means of transportation – it gives you a freedom and mobility that make life very exciting. In Los Angeles in the future we may have electric cars, or smaller cars, but it's wholly unrealistic to think of creating an environment where people aren't going to drive anywhere. In my view, it's not going to happen.

JS: Do you find that you are getting increasingly involved in the public realm, in contrast with your work in the past, which has been mostly residential?

FI: We are interested in transferring our efforts into the public realm. We're doing two buildings at UCLA: one is presently under construction, the other, the addition to the Southern Regional Library, will start on site this spring. There's the UC Riverside project I talked about earlier, as well as our competition entry for an addition to the Getty Museum, the Herculaneum Villa, which is very much a public building. But at the same time, I have to say that houses give you an opportunity to experiment with ideas, forms and new methods of construction that you just don't get in a public project.

JS: There are far more restrictions in public buildings, aren't there?

FI: In some cases, but I still think that designing a house is the hardest thing. So many of the spaces are different, you don't have repetition to play with. The relationship you form with the client for the house is also quite intense. This sets up the strongest challenges: there are more expectations to be met. In public buildings, the relationship doesn't tend to be so strong, although I can think of some exceptions. For example, the relationship that Frank Gehry has formed with Ernest Fleischmann and others at the Disney Concert Hall has been a major influence in putting together the design. There's also the relationship that Kahn had with Salk, and that IM Pei had with Mitterand on the Louvre projects.

With public buildings, the client may be very powerful. But with a house, the relationship between the architect and client is more intimate, more provocative.

JS: At this point in your career and the development of your office, you're attracting increased international attention and, with it, some opportunities to build outside of LA.

FI: We're keen to expand our field of work. Right now we're working on the Bunka Shutter project in Tokyo, which is a large urban design scheme with an office building attached. We're also designing a housing project in The Hague. In addition, there's the prospect of a project outside of Paris; a large park where visitors come on public transport to explore the edge of the city.

JS: We've talked a bit about how you see the work of your office evolving. What do you think is going to happen to LA as a whole? How do you see the future of architecture here?

FI: The future kind of eludes us all, yet everyone's curious about it. Right now, landscape design is becoming very important and I think that in the future it will play a major role in the architecture of the city. A case in point is the new Getty Center that Richard Meier is designing in Brentwood. When I look at the scheme, I think of the things that I learned when I worked for Jaquelin Robertson as senior architect on the Shahestan Pahlavi project in Tehran. Prior to the fall of the Shah, we developed a master plan for a new capital city that celebrated the relationship of architecture to the landscape, as well as the positioning of buildings in relation to one another to create a strong urban fabric. What I found when I lived in Tehran, which is in some ways very similar to LA, is that you don't build on top of a hill, for if you do, the hillside starts to erode. If you're going to build in a strong topographical location, you build down in the valley or in a ravine or canyon.

Of course, Meier's Getty Center project negates this. It sits on top of a hill overlooking the freeway. A large portion of the budget has gone into securing the site for construction. I don't mean to criticise Meier for the siting of his 'Acropolis'. In fact, the buildings that are now going up are rich and exciting pieces of architecture. Compositionally, they form another city within this city – an enclave on a hill. They reaffirm the ideal of Los Angeles: to be separatist, isolated and protected from the elements. But here that is impossible to achieve. The forces of nature are always at work and the architecture we create cannot tame them, it can only adjust itself and be tempered by our hand.

JS: This brings us back full circle, to the discussion about the landscape and the climate and how architecture in the past related to it but does no longer, because of the 'cities within', the move to build defensible architecture. Basically, I think you're the one architect in this area who has a special kind of sensitivity to the landscape, and this makes your work quite different.

FI: I would agree with you on that one.

P10 AND P14: Virgin Records

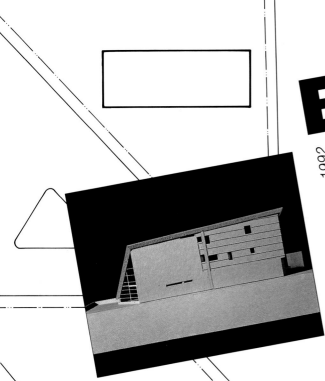

BALDWIN RESIDENCE

1992

This two-family beach house in Venice pays homage to the sea with its folding plane roof of anodised titanium panels. Reflecting the shimmering light of the nearby ocean, it forms an allegorical connection to its site – a sweeping, iridescent wave.

The folded plane starts at the ground plane, but as it develops in plan, and reverberates in section and elevation, a variety of architectural situations unfolds.

In elevation this house declares two very different scales. The front is shielded, providing protection and security; the back opens and accommodates a two-storey volume terracing to a garden below. The dynamic of the ocean and city has been carefully measured, and a home and an urban refuge created.

Venice, California

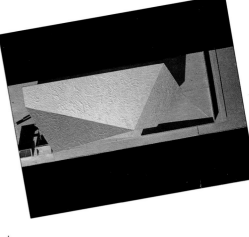

LEFT: Site plan; *P20, FROM ABOVE*: Side elevation, front elevation, second level, longitudinal section; *P21, FROM ABOVE*: Side elevation, rear elevation, third level, cross sections

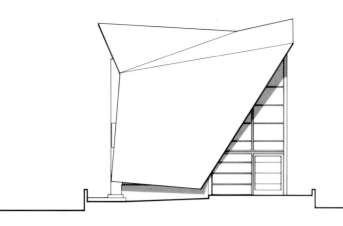

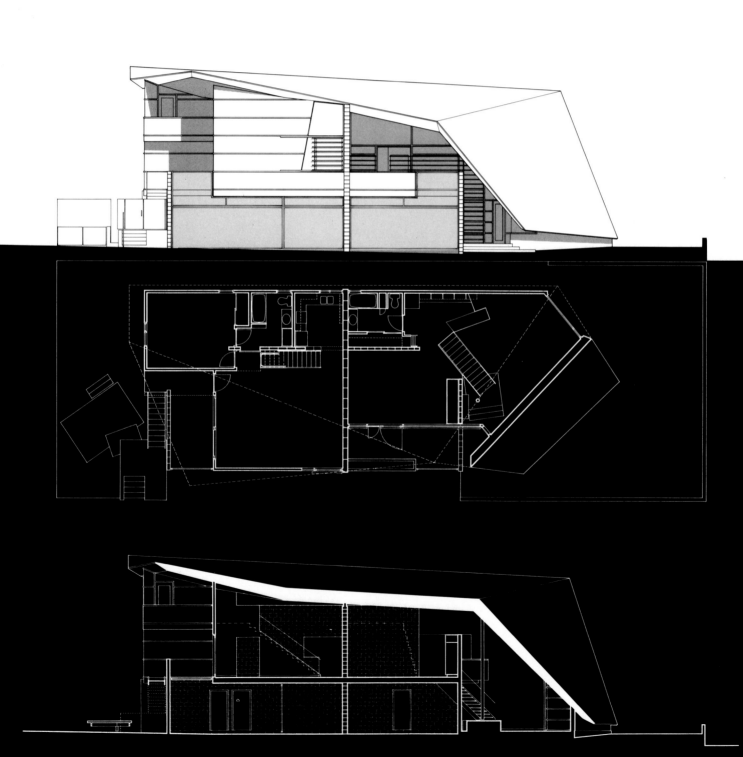

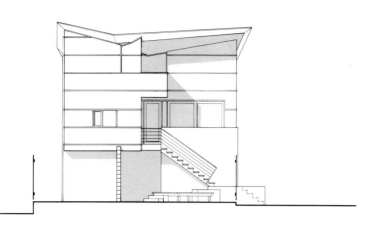

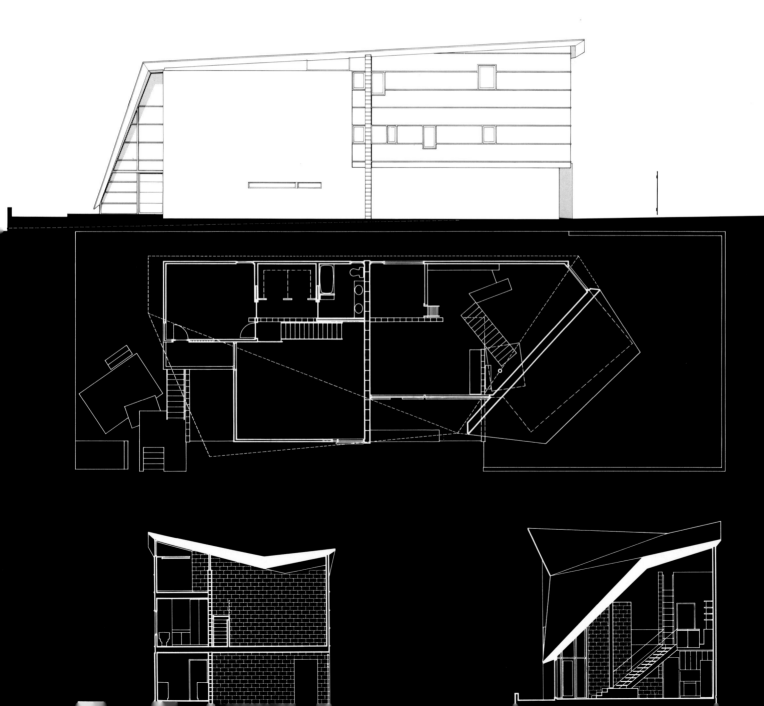

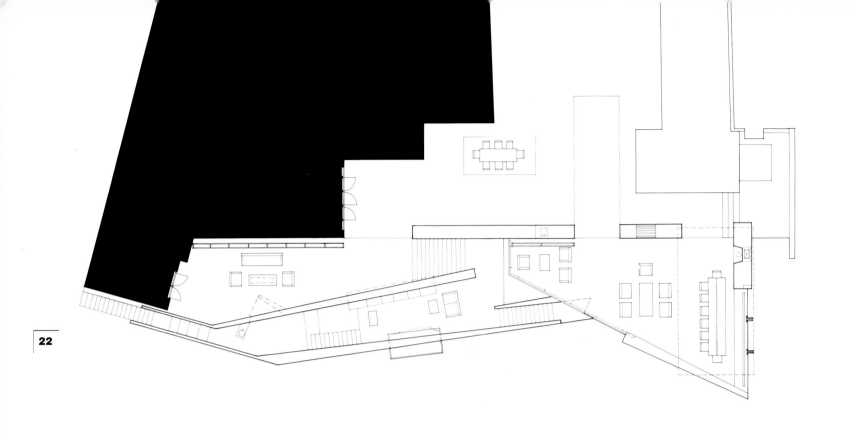

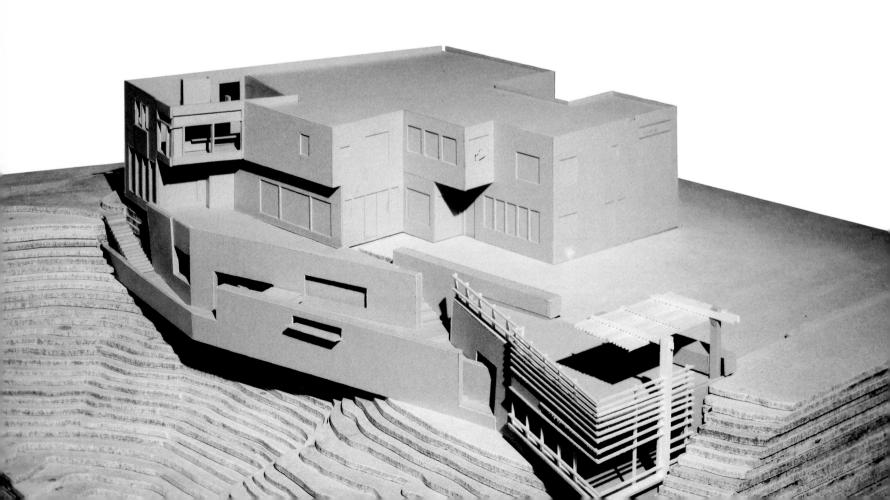

BELLDEGRUN HOUSE

○○1993

Shaped as a retaining wall to a hillside in Brentwood, California, this guest house also forms a terrace off the rear yard of the original structure. Not a pavilion in a garden like the Woo House, but a platform set into the site, it pulls itself out, commanding views of the canyon beyond.

Programmatically, this building celebrates the expanding needs of a growing family, but with a twist. The clients, who are of Finnish-Israeli descent, asked the architects to celebrate their heritage by including a sauna directly linked to the pool, and a wine-tasting room as part of the wine cellar. Other inclusions are a gymnasium and additional bedroom for the eldest son.

Brentwood, California

LEFT: Terrace level; *ABOVE*: Lower level; *P24*: Front elevation; *P25*: Cross section.

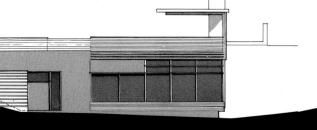

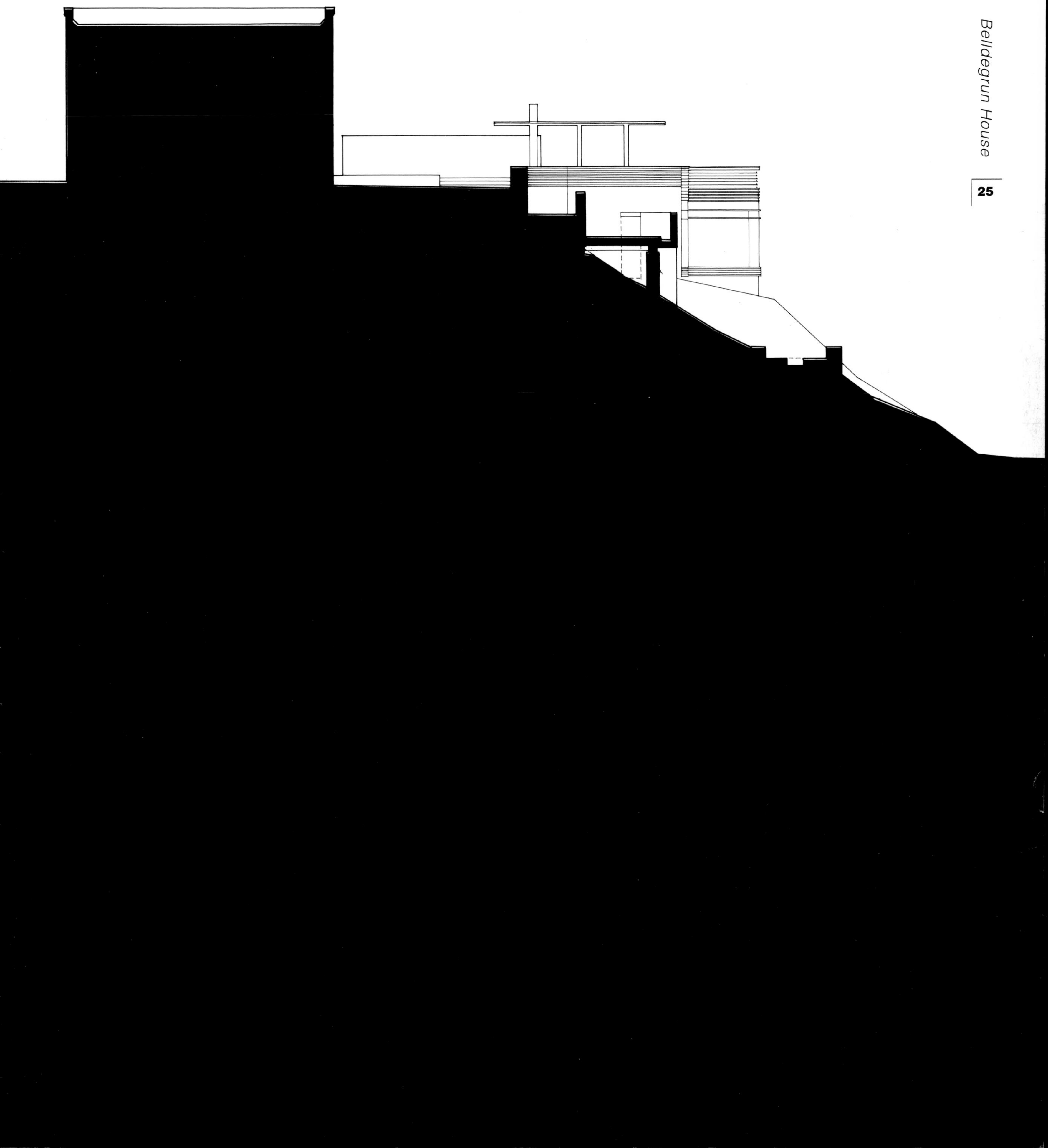

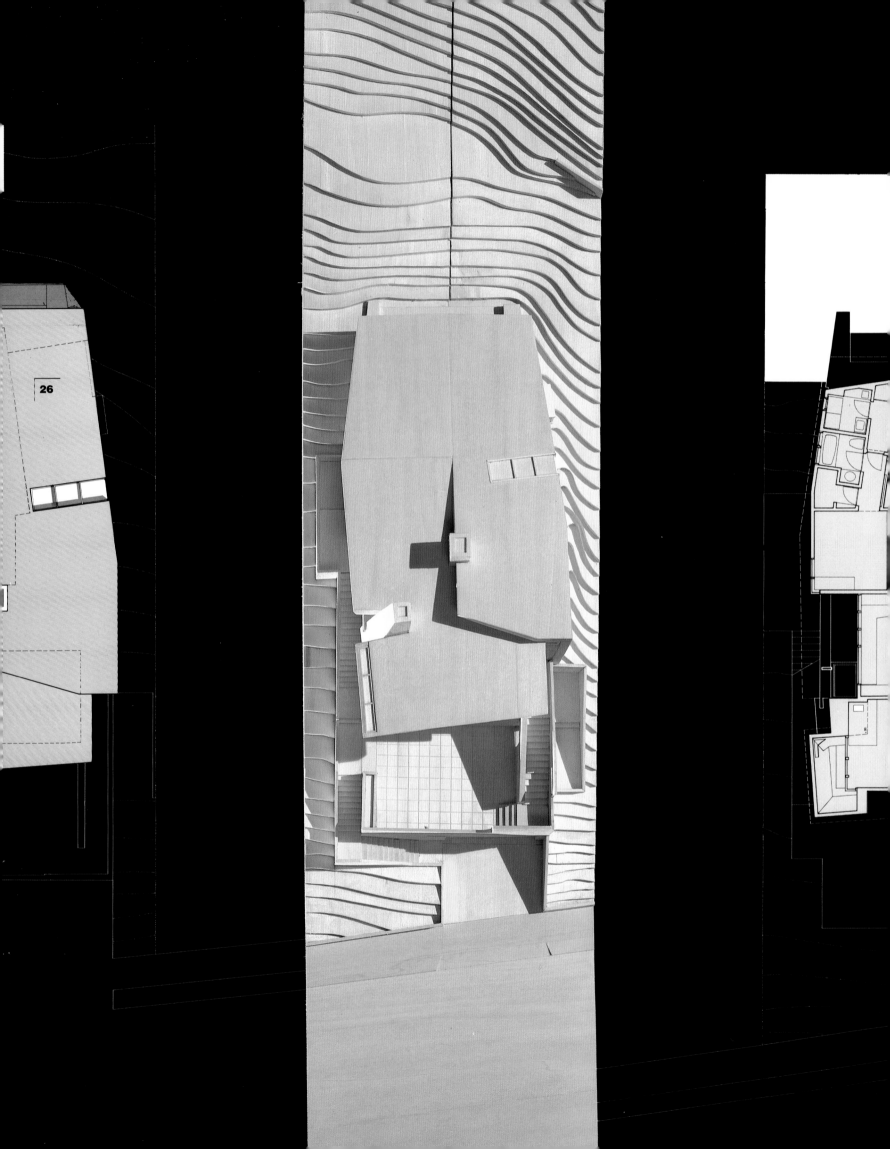

26

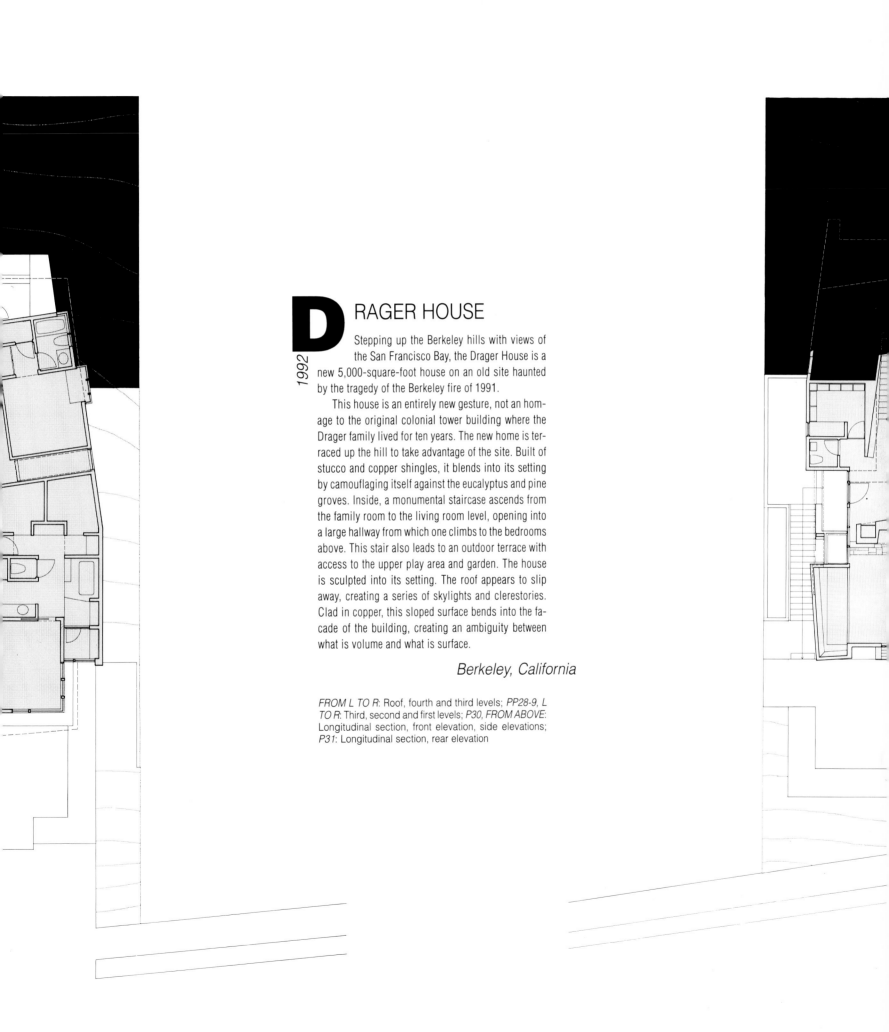

DRAGER HOUSE

1992

Stepping up the Berkeley hills with views of the San Francisco Bay, the Drager House is a new 5,000-square-foot house on an old site haunted by the tragedy of the Berkeley fire of 1991.

This house is an entirely new gesture, not an homage to the original colonial tower building where the Drager family lived for ten years. The new home is terraced up the hill to take advantage of the site. Built of stucco and copper shingles, it blends into its setting by camouflaging itself against the eucalyptus and pine groves. Inside, a monumental staircase ascends from the family room to the living room level, opening into a large hallway from which one climbs to the bedrooms above. This stair also leads to an outdoor terrace with access to the upper play area and garden. The house is sculpted into its setting. The roof appears to slip away, creating a series of skylights and clerestories. Clad in copper, this sloped surface bends into the facade of the building, creating an ambiguity between what is volume and what is surface.

Berkeley, California

FROM L TO R: Roof, fourth and third levels; *PP28-9, L TO R*: Third, second and first levels; *P30, FROM ABOVE*: Longitudinal section, front elevation, side elevations; *P31*: Longitudinal section, rear elevation

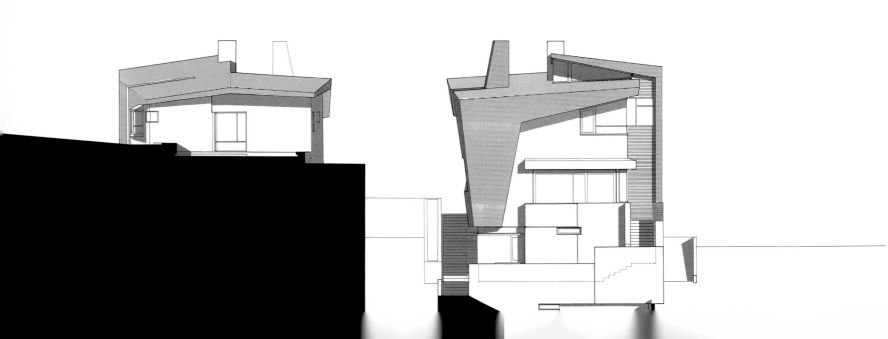

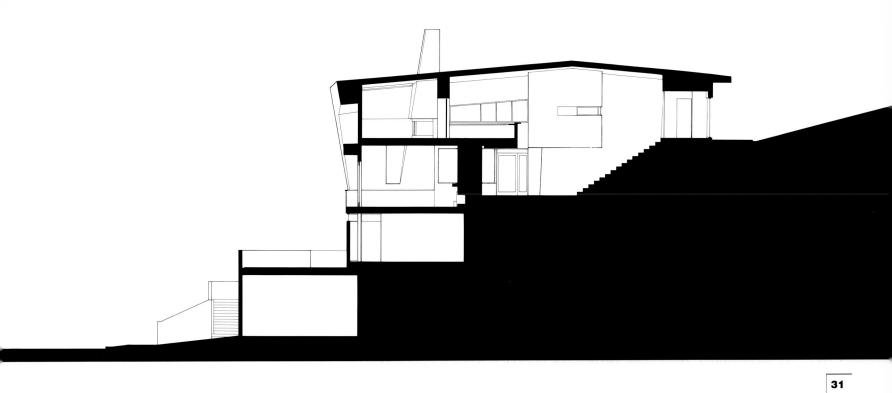

JUPITER HOUSE

1993

The new house designed for a retired couple from Philadelphia acknowledges its proximity to the sea in several ways. The major spaces all open towards views of the intracoastal waterway. The master bedroom resembles a ship's mast at the top of the roof. The roof itself, like that of the Venice Beach Baldwin Residence, is reminiscent of a grand wave suspended in a state of active relief. It crowns the composition of all the major spaces in the house, pinning itself down to the ground in a large, undulating screened-in porch.

Entry into the house is through a large vehicular court which contains a garage stairway, a Banyan tree, and pools. From here, one encounters a monumental wall which divides the public rooms of the house from a service corridor. This wall will be used as a giant armature to exhibit the clients' extensive collection of folk art. It also contains a stairway and elevator.

The house extends orthogonally towards the intercoastal waterway. The linear thrust of the plan is carried into a series of exterior spaces: a screened-in porch, a patio, and the pool and pool deck.

The materials were chosen for their appropriateness to the beach. The roof is to be constructed of glued-lam beams, covered in lead-coated copper. The monumental wall is of coral stone, and major volumes of the house will be veneered in plaster.

Jupiter, Florida

LEFT: Preliminary sketch; PP34-5: First level; PP36-7: composite plans/sections; P38: Second level; P39: Third level; P41: Front and side elevations

pool within

living

waterway

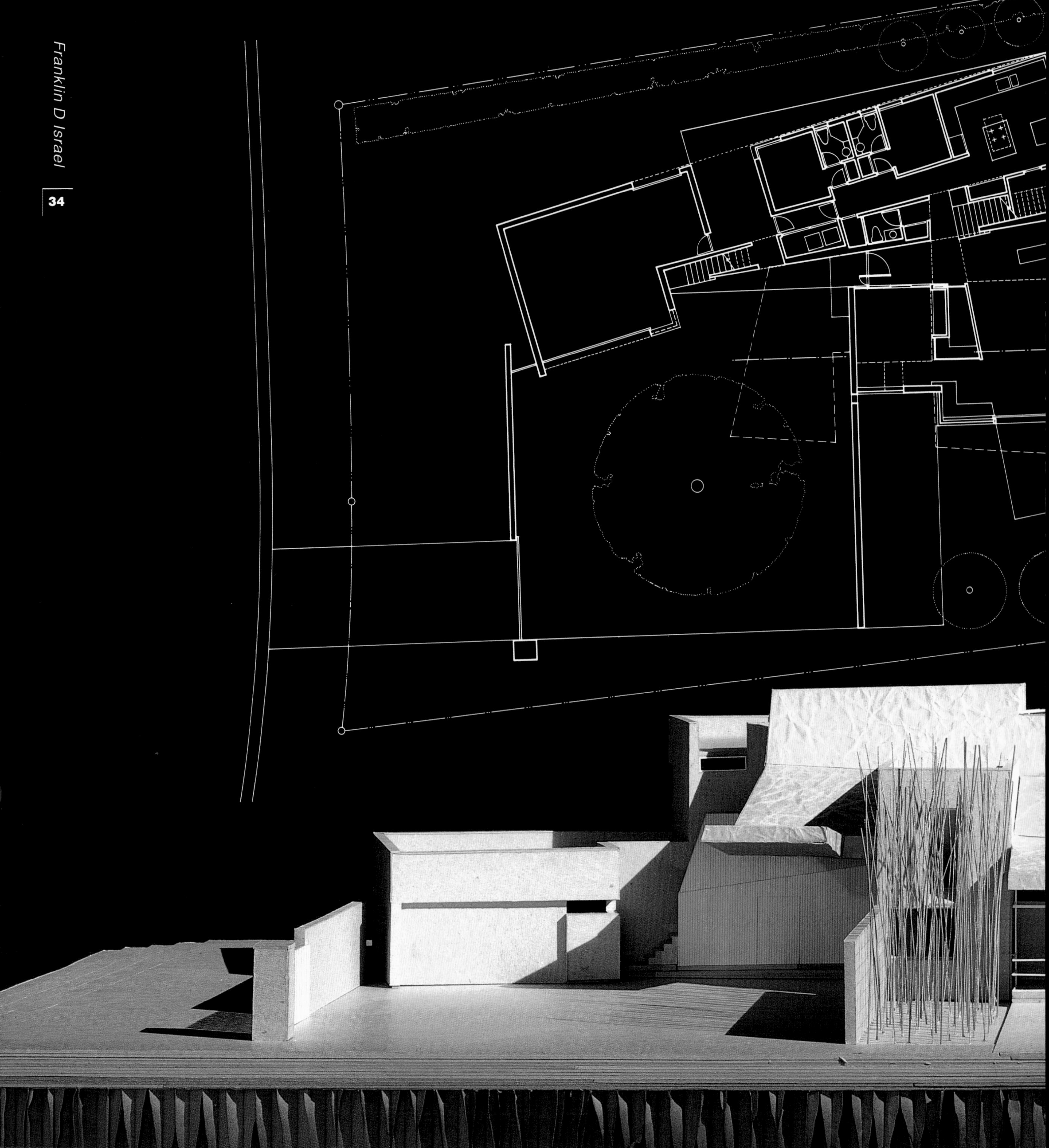

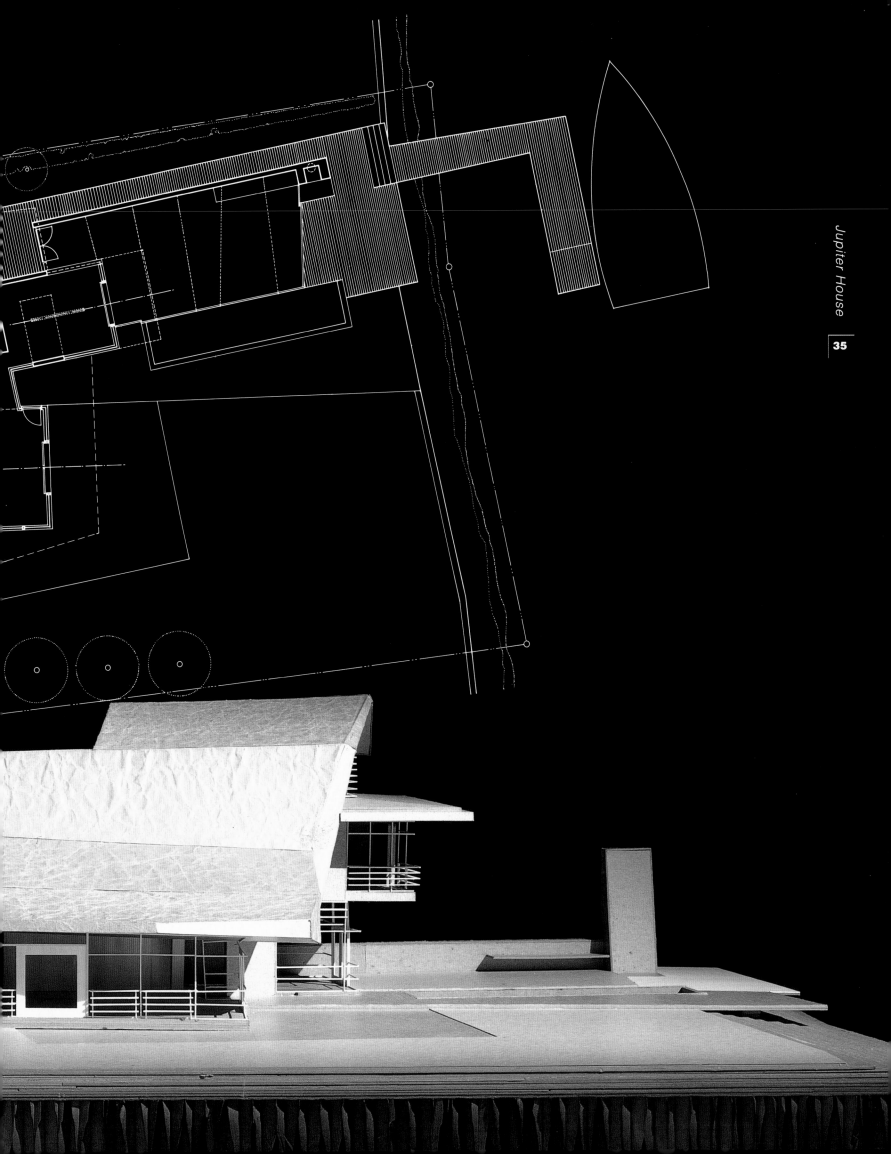

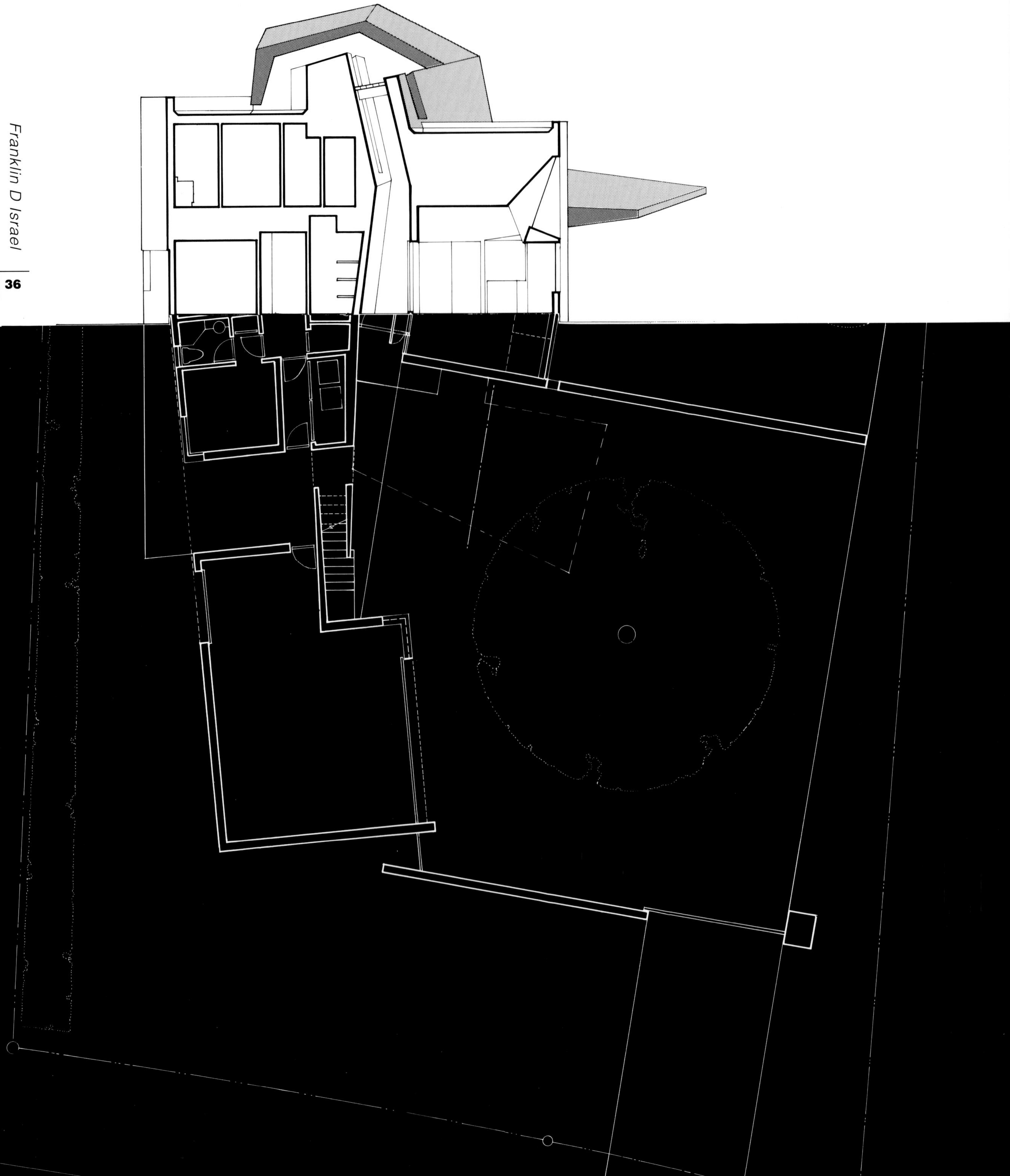

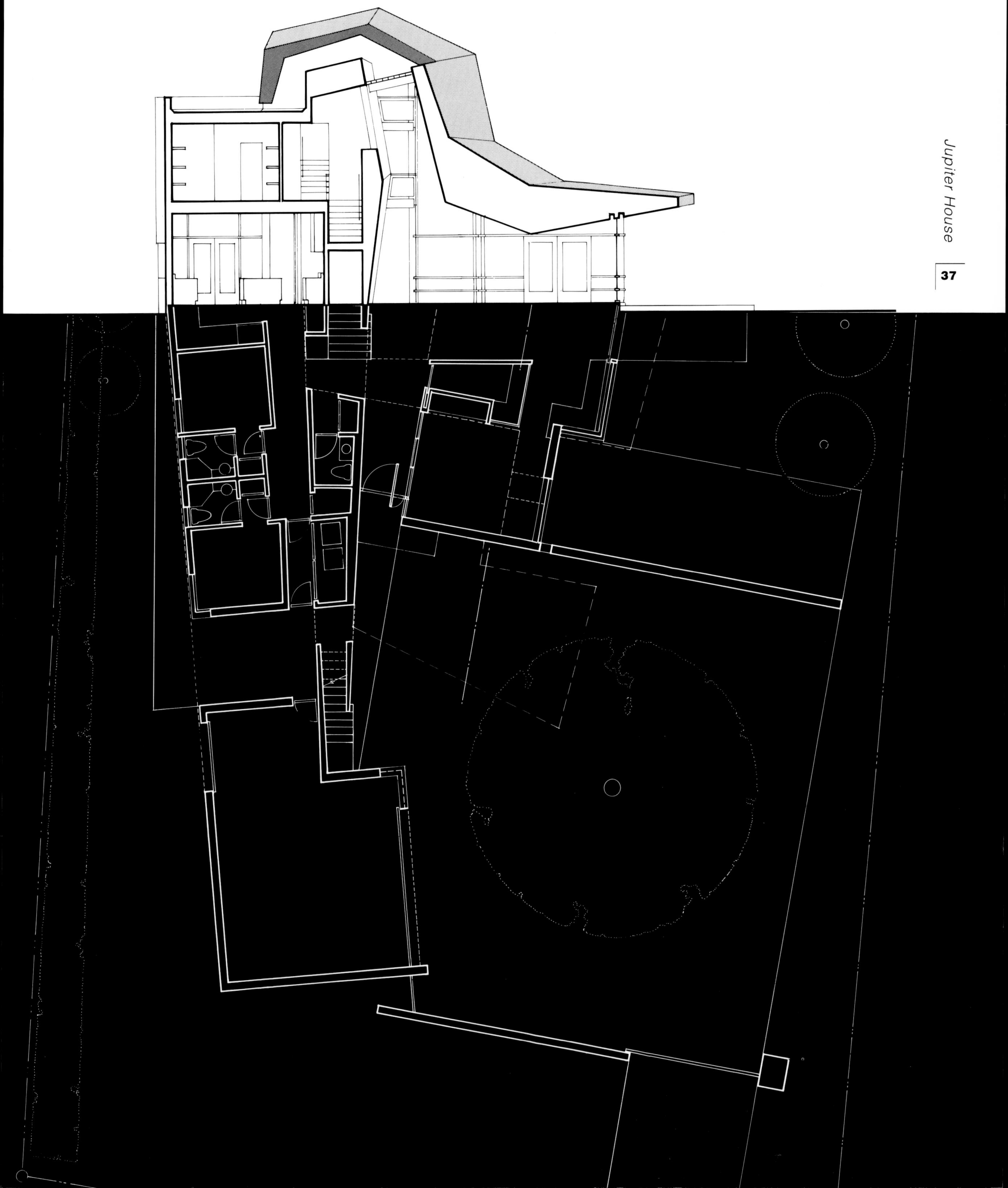

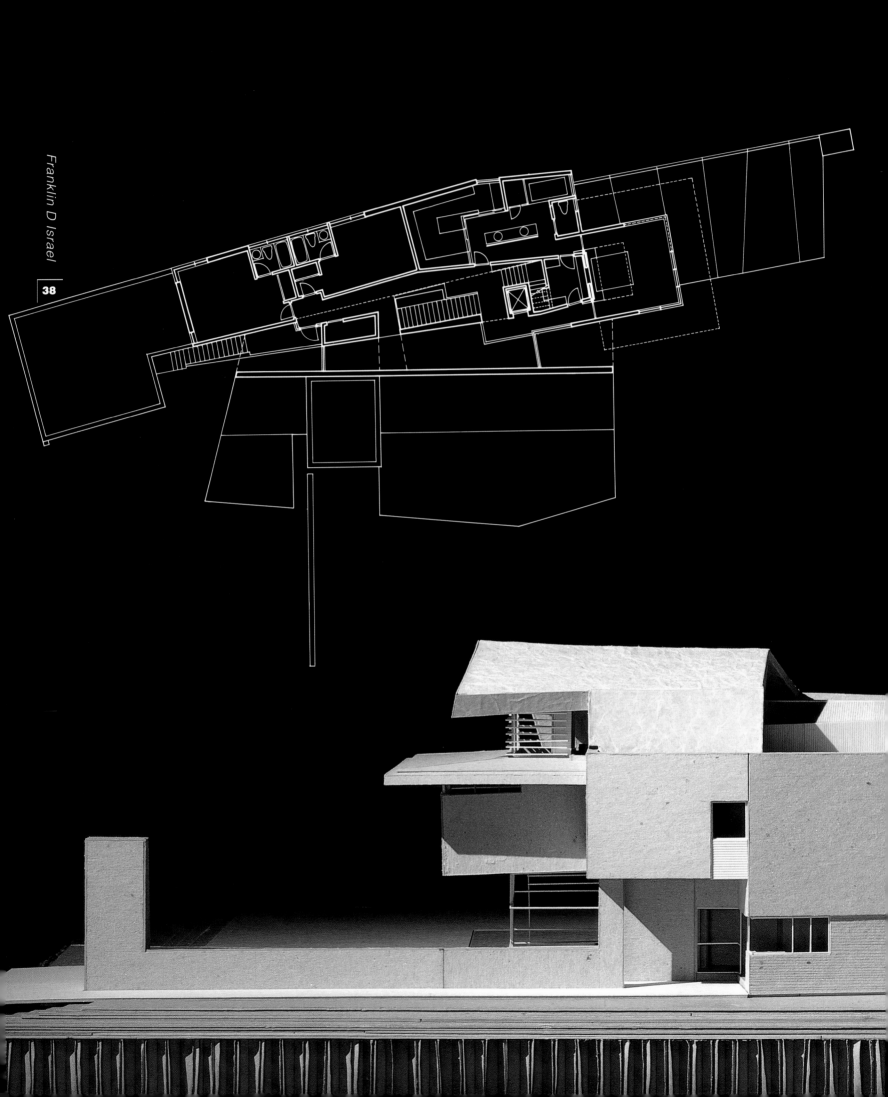

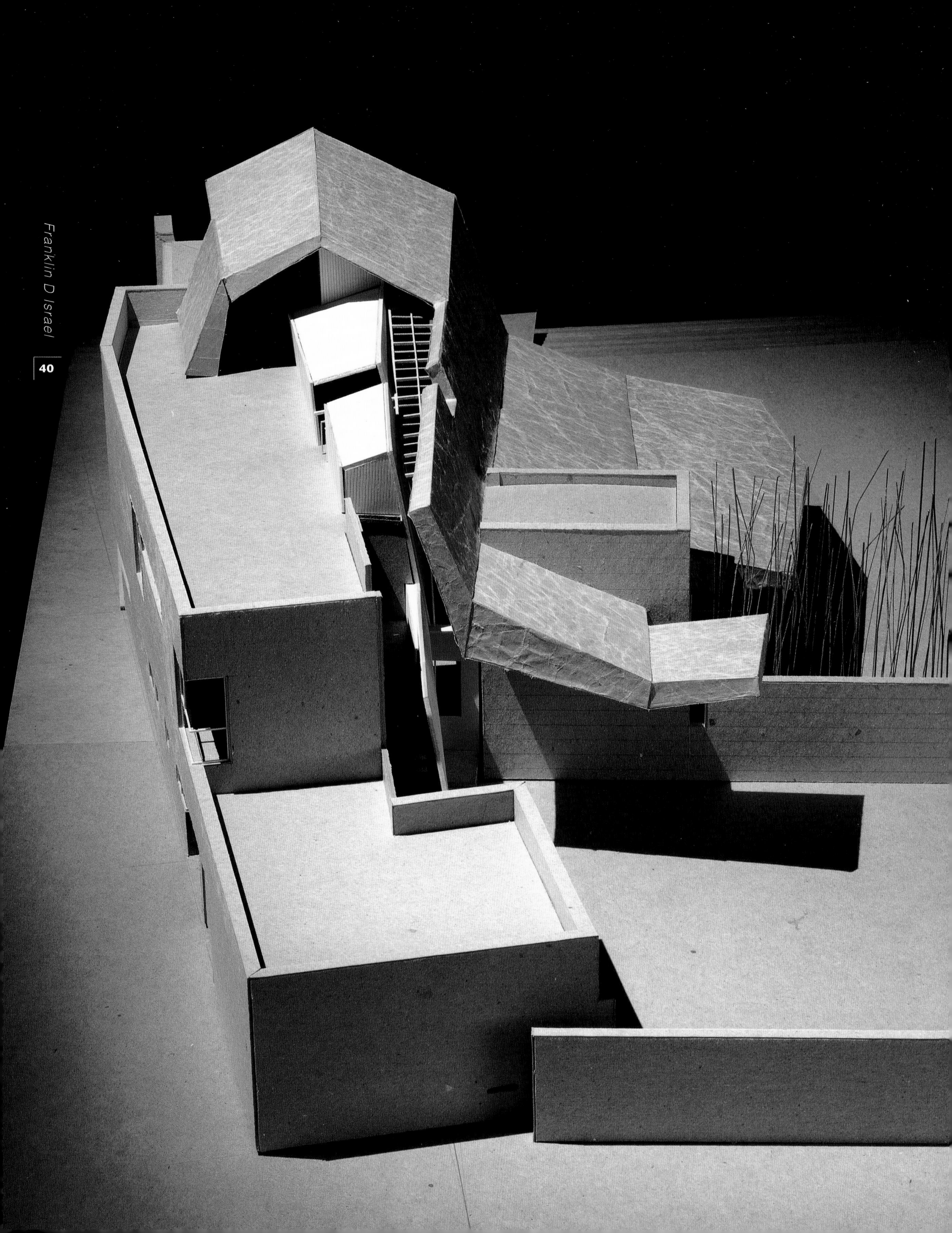

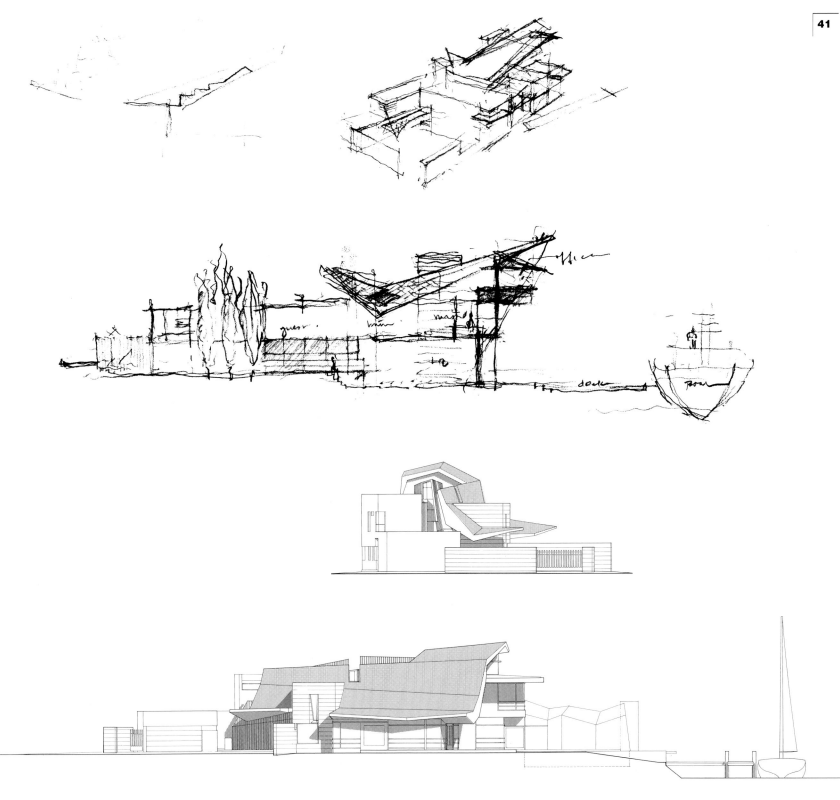

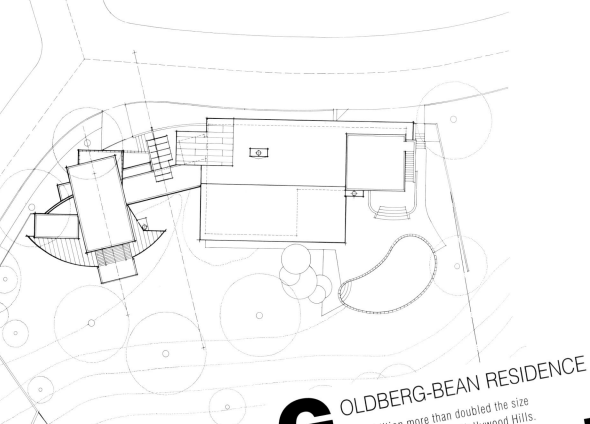

GOLDBERG-BEAN RESIDENCE

1991

This addition more than doubled the size of an existing house in the Hollywood Hills. The Goldberg–Bean residence is a 1950s ranch style building set in a quiet residential neighbourhood, on a curved, gently sloping site graced with magnificent oak trees and spectacular views. The clients asked us to remodel the existing house while adding a private realm that completely transforms the site, projecting a series of dramatically articulated three-dimensional volumes beyond the original house into the garden.

Linking the new with the old, a ninety-foot-long undulating plaster wall both invites and denies communication between the public and private spaces. Set around the curve of the wall and the site, both the old and the new wings focus on the distant views.

Spaces within the home are delineated through structural and sculptural elements – a studio is elevated on four posts which form the canopy chamber for a bed below, and a telescoping cone of steel forms a fireplace that functions as an eddy within the spatial flow.

The materials reinforce the variety of forms. A gridded rectilinear studio perched at the top of the site is covered in cedar plywood with redwood battens. The master bedroom has curved walls and a skewed, vaulted roof, all clad with bonderised sheet metal panels. Service areas are finished in metal-trowelled plaster. Tongue-and-groove wooden siding on the street facade recalls the existing lapped siding of house and fence.

Entry is signified by a small pool-shaped garden – a gesture of welcome in the arid Los Angeles climate. A tilting steel and glass canopy shades the street terrace and the visitor. The entry also serves as the centre of movement through the site – a place from which one can proceed to the garden or the house, to a formal or informal order, to a public or private domain.

Hollywood, California

ABOVE: Site plan; PP46-7: Sketches and longitudinal section/elevation; PP52-3, FROM ABOVE: First level, composite plans/sections; PP54-5: Second level; P57, FROM ABOVE: Rear elevation, front elevation

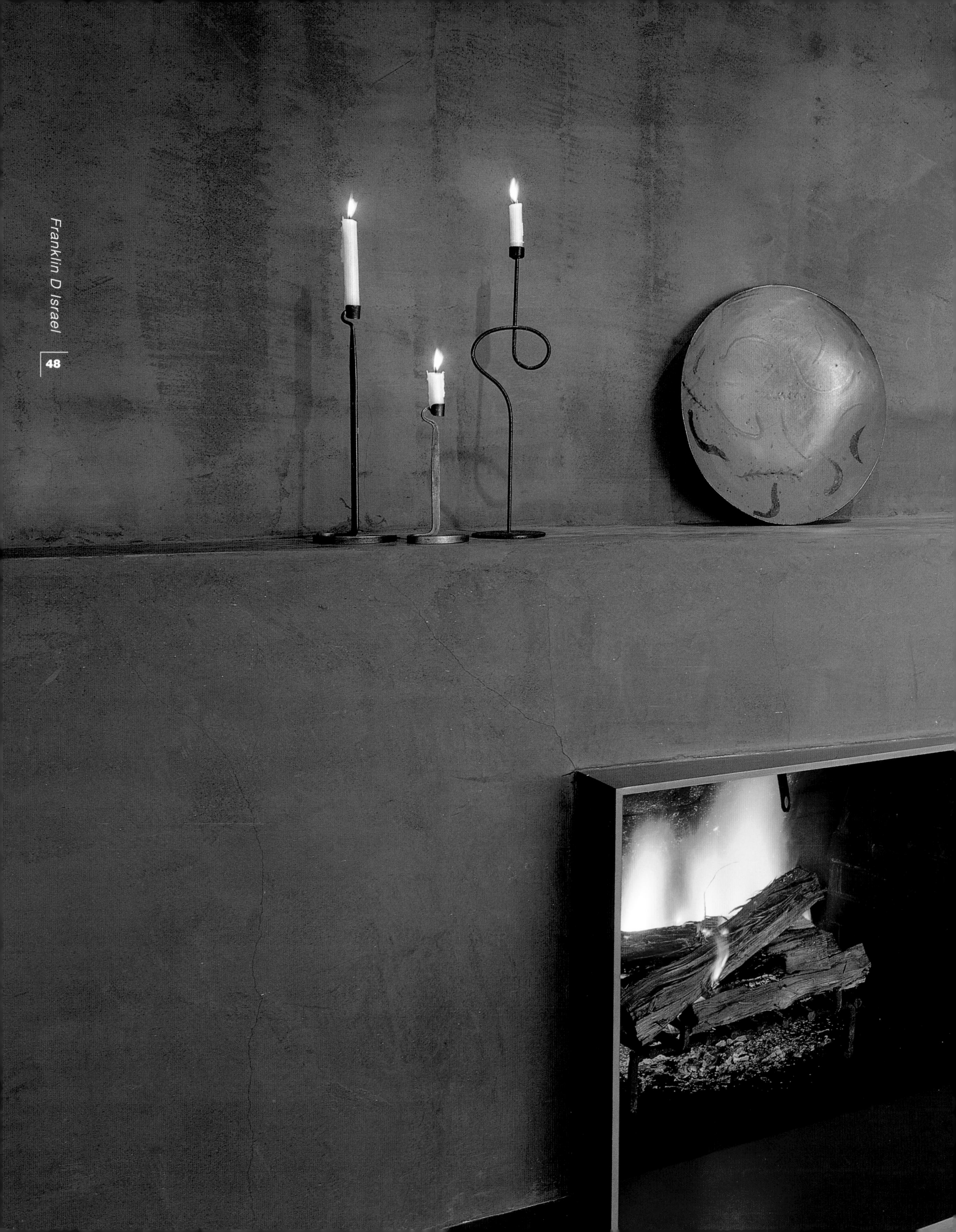

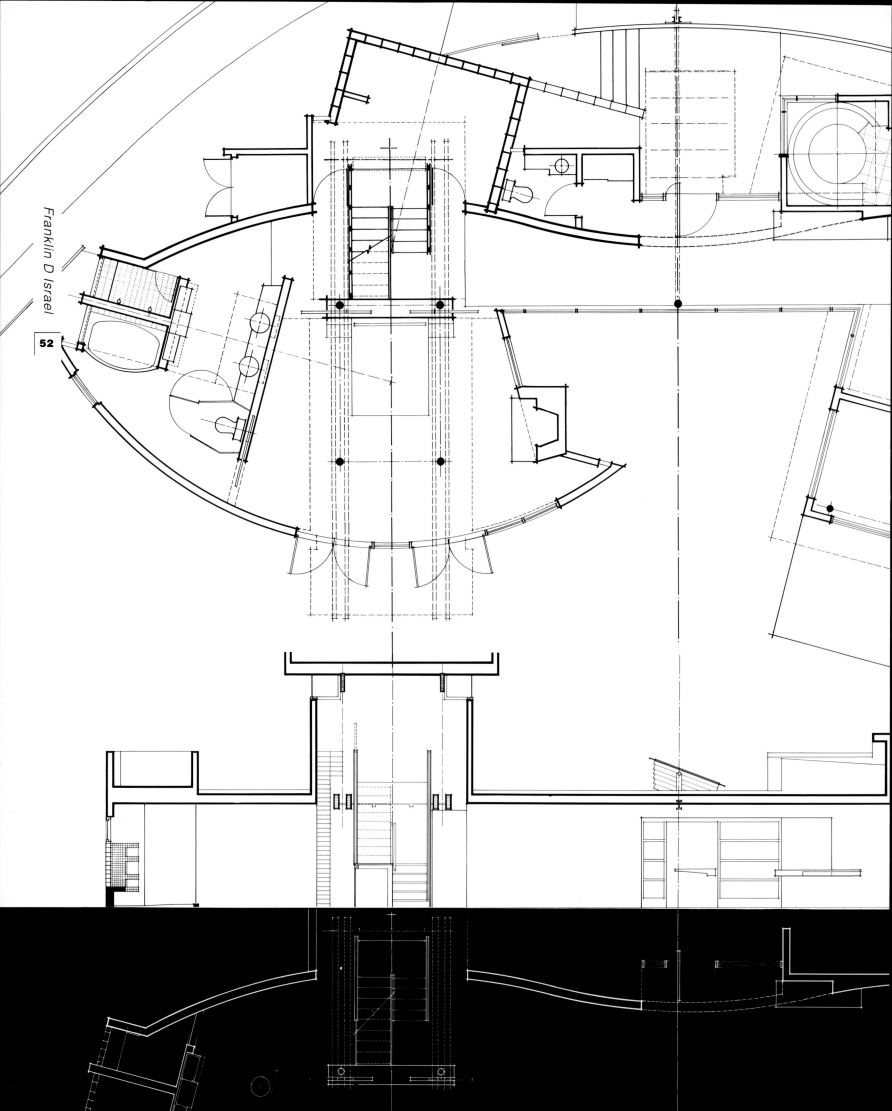

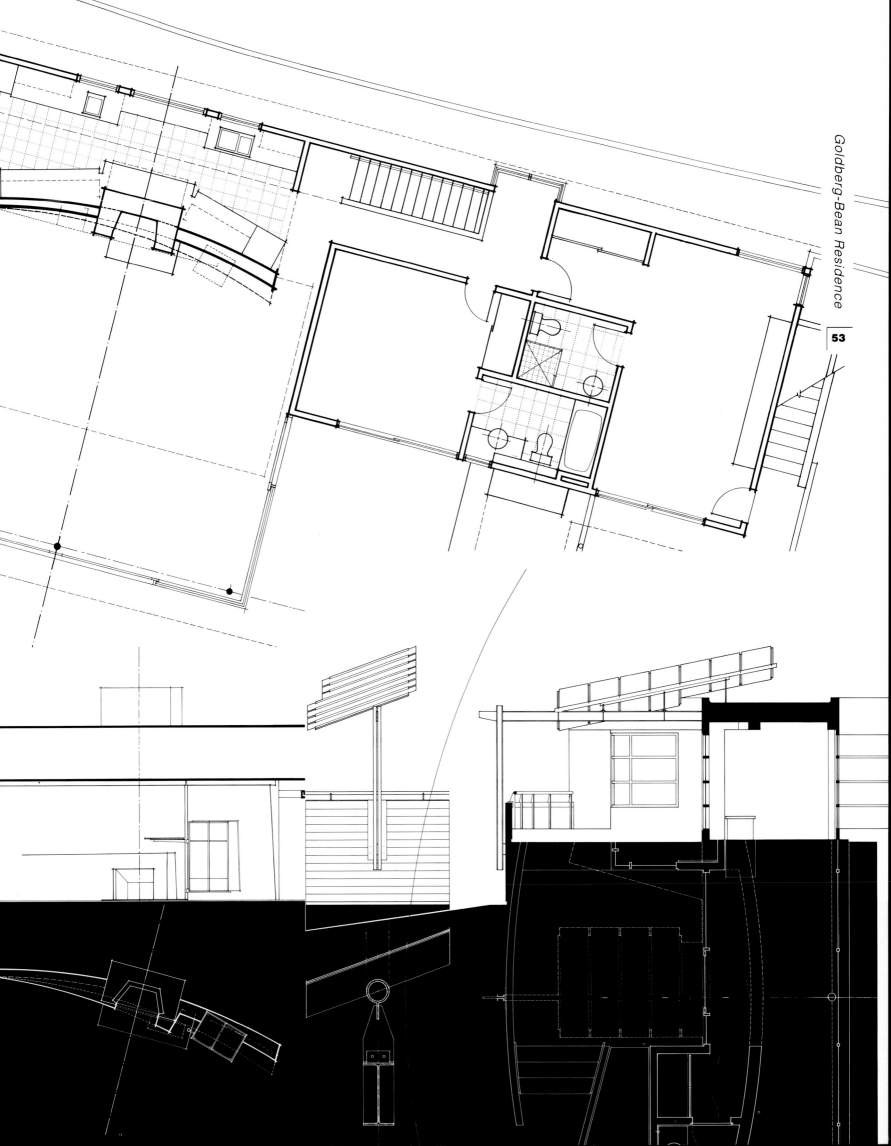

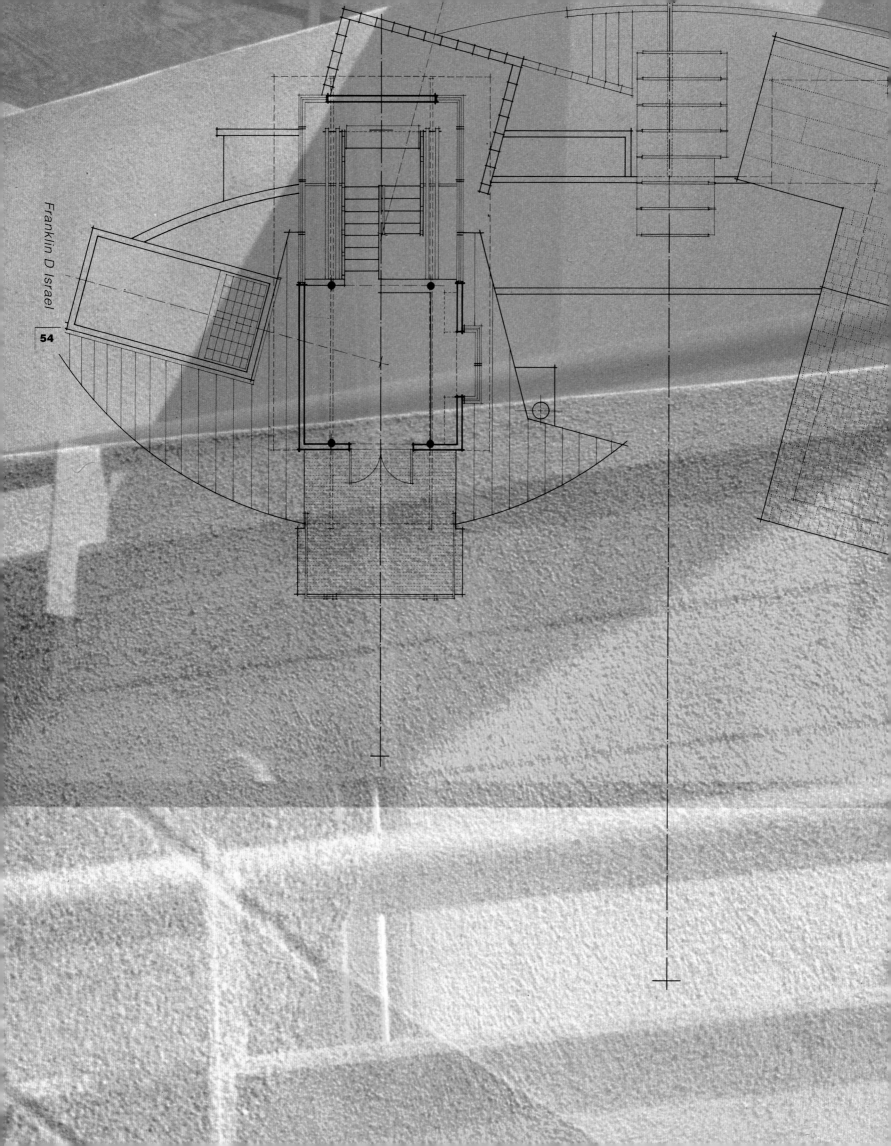

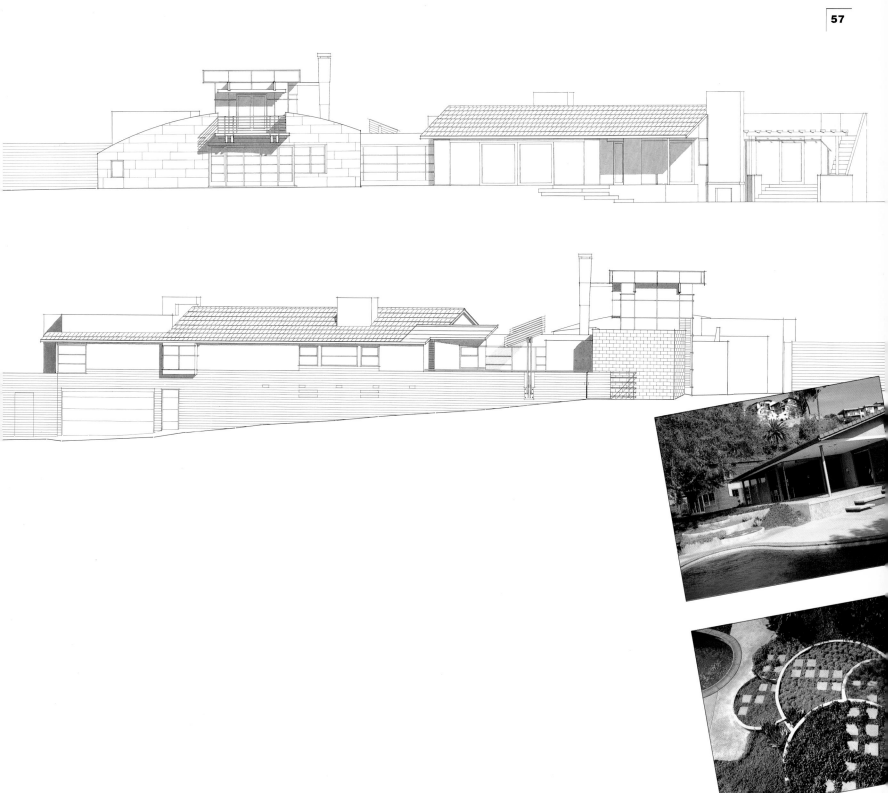

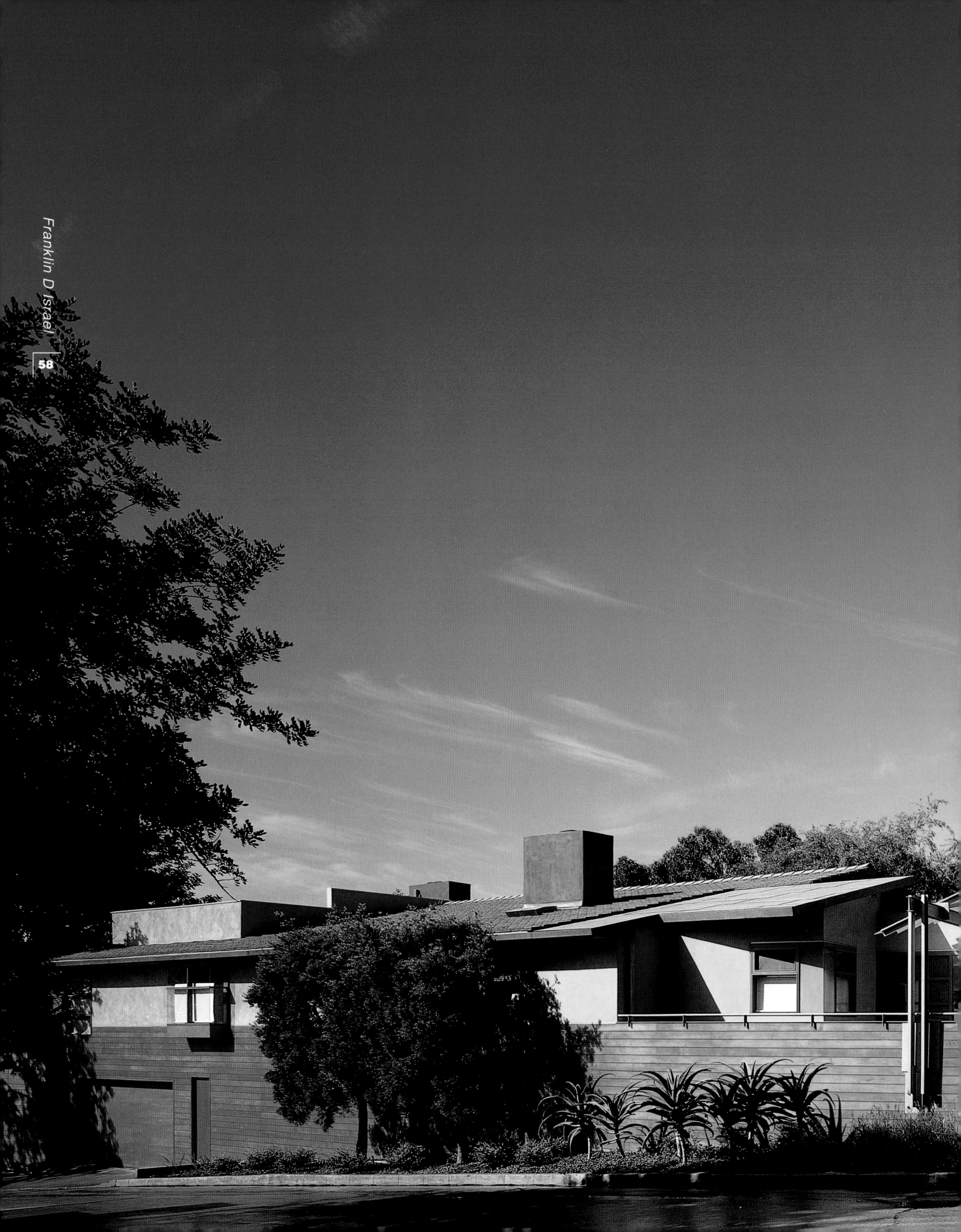

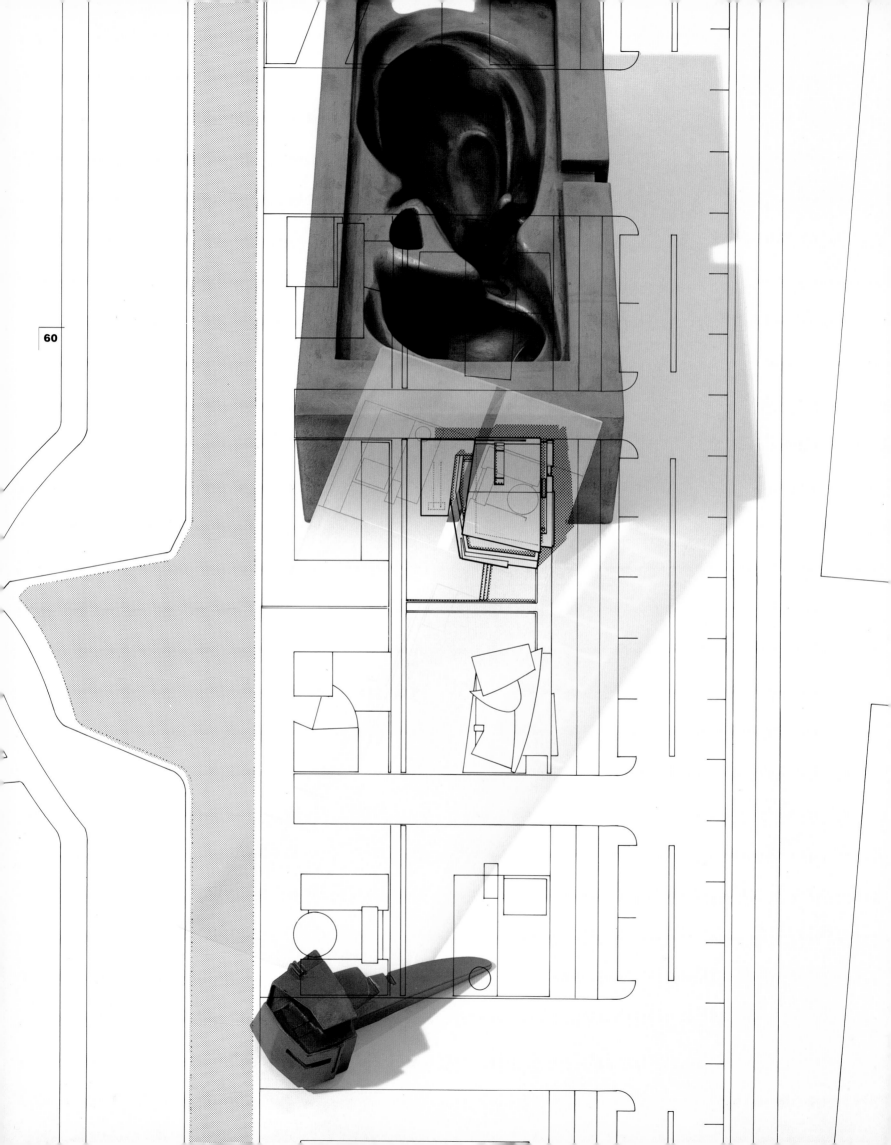

HAGUE I

1992

This small 1,800-square-foot house is one of eight detached garden houses to be built in a suburban area of The Hague. Organised on five separate levels, the house opens up at the ground level to a garden. From there it winds around from the entry to the rear facade, with a stepped terrace connecting the various bedroom levels. Upon entering, a small vestibule provides a place to discard one's boots. The entry path then leads along a walkway to the kitchen and dining area. Below, the living room opens out onto the garden through large picture windows. The studio above is a suspended platform which looks down upon the living area. Two levels of bedrooms occupy the upper portion of the building.

Built of brick, steel, and wood, the house pays homage to the early twentieth-century garden cottages at Park Meerwijk. These somewhat idiosyncratic buildings combine a wide assortment of materials within a set of garden pavilions that resemble chess pieces on a contoured board.

The Netherlands

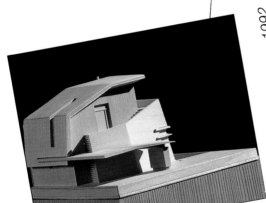

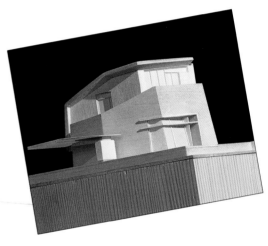

LEFT: Site plan; P63, FROM ABOVE: Fifth, fourth, third and first/second levels; P64, FROM ABOVE: Northwest elevation, section AA, southwest elevation; P65; FROM ABOVE: Northeast elevation, section BB, southeast elevation

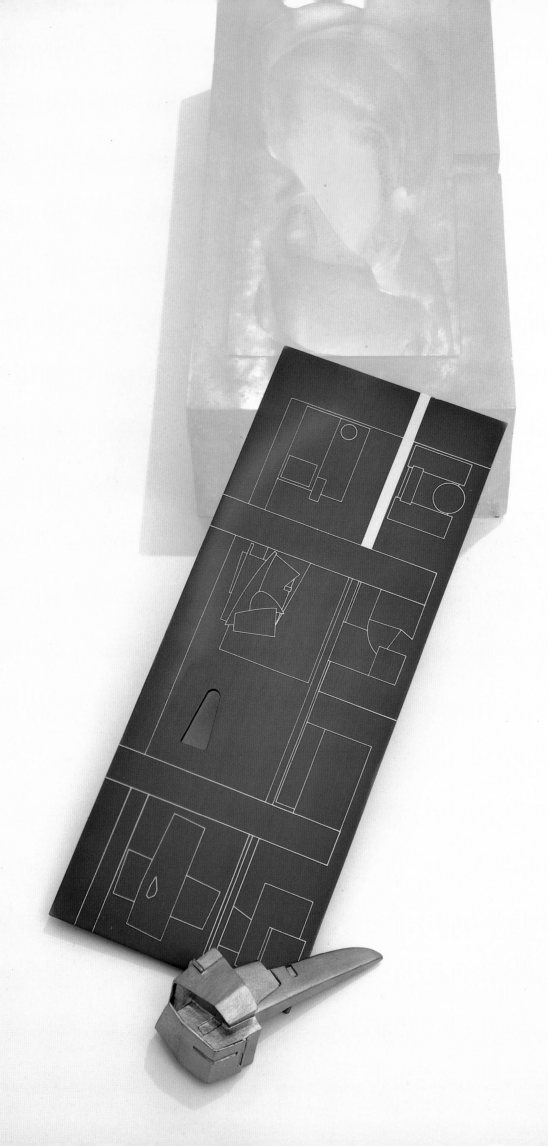

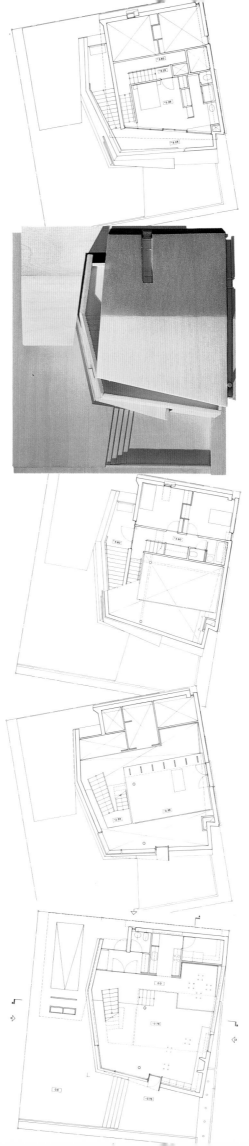

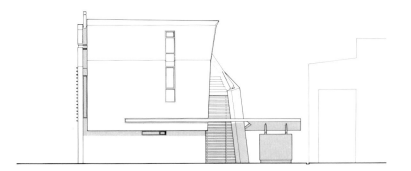

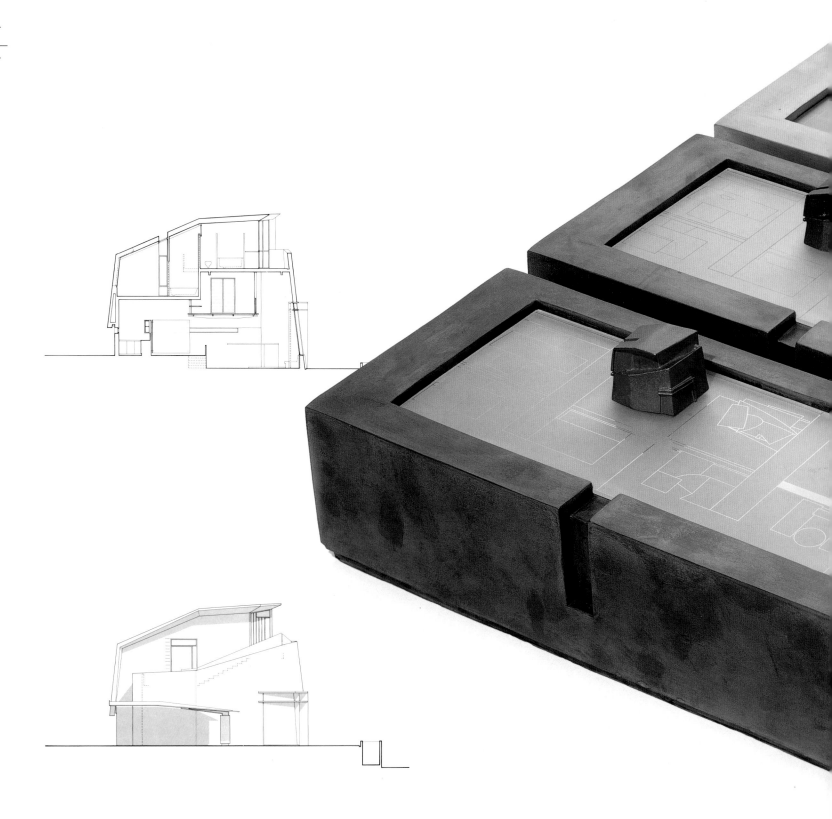

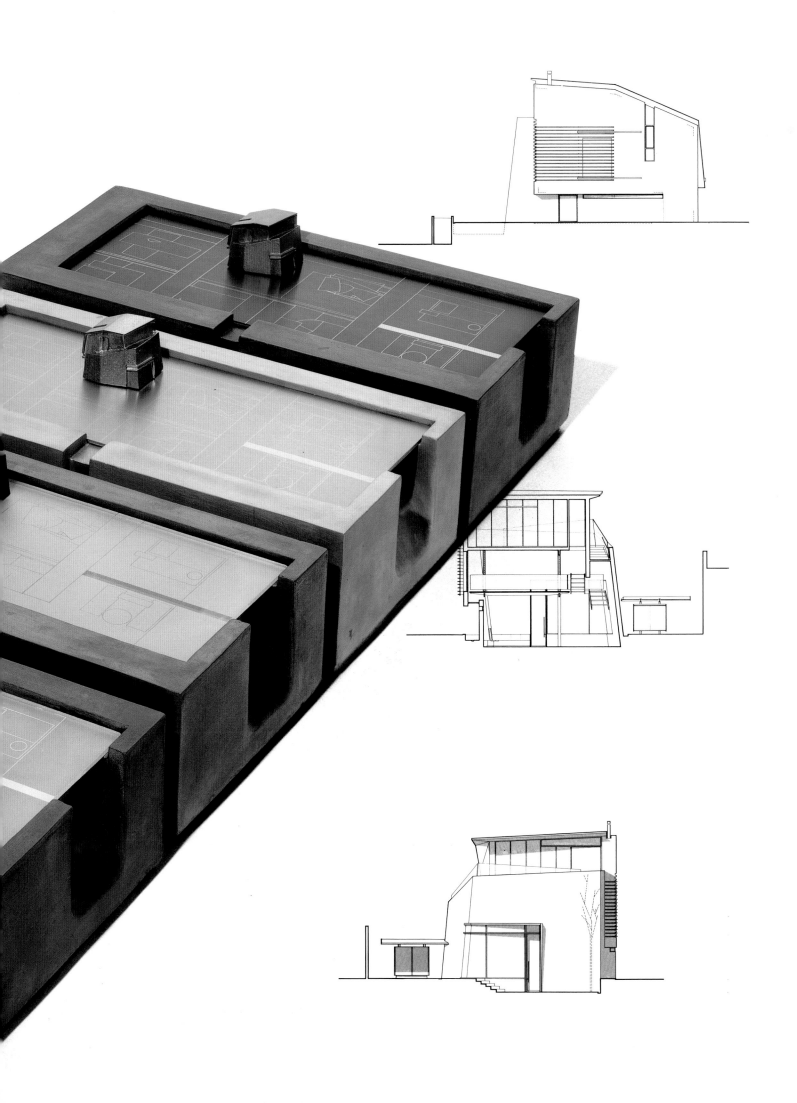

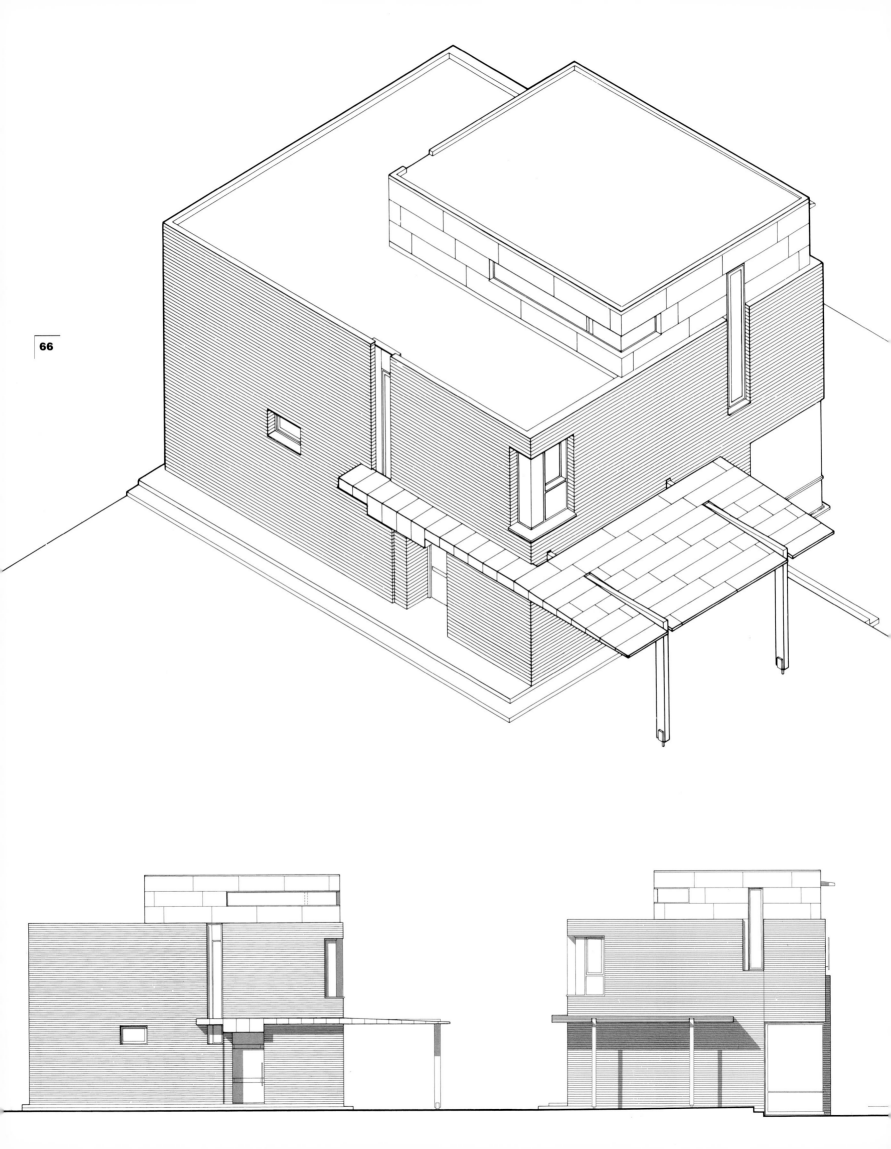

S PARTAN HOUSE

1992

This house celebrates the De Stijl movement, forming a series of orthogonal planes that are interlocked in plan and elevation. It is a second, more spartan version of the programme which is presented on the previous pages, modified in response to budgetary constraints.

The house is arranged on three levels, with the master bedroom at the top looking out towards the garden at the rear. Below, are situated two additional bedrooms, and at ground level the living/dining space and kitchen. These more public rooms open up to one another and eventually extend through a series of large doors to the garden.

Ochre-coloured brick will be used, with steel fenestration and a zinc shingled roof.

The Hague, Netherlands

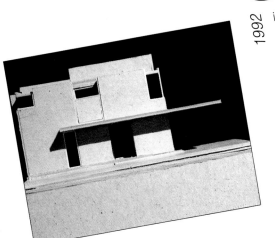

ABOVE LEFT: Axonometric; *BELOW L TO R*: Front, side, rear and side elevations; *P68*: First level; *P69, FROM ABOVE*: Second level, third level

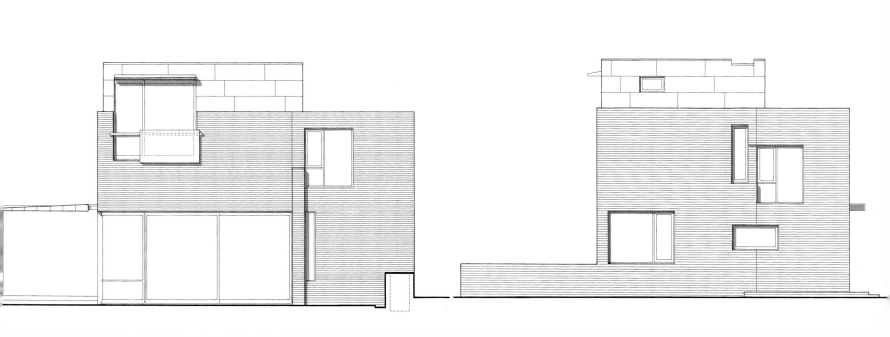

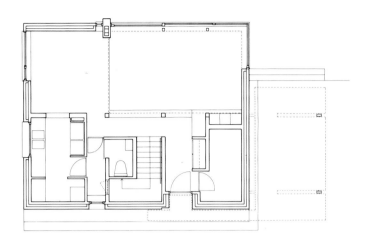

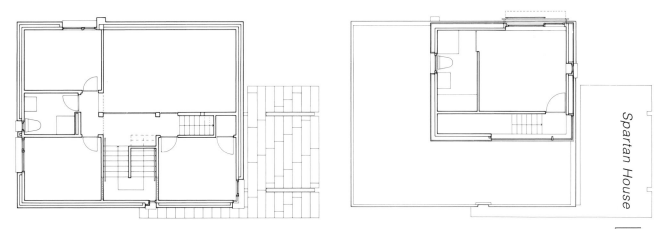

WOO FONG PAVILION

1992

This structure comprises a 1,400-square-foot addition to a bungalow situated on the north side of Silver Lake.

The clients needed to expand the home, principally to contain their extensive book collection and to provide additional sleeping spaces. The solution connects these two concerns with hundreds of feet of bookshelves integrated into a dramatic passageway to the new pavilion – a literary as well as literal passageway.

A new axis cuts a swath from the existing house to the addition at a conservatively oblique angle, preserving the existing structure save for a patio and pergola at the front of the house and some modifications to the streetside garage. The addition creates two new bedrooms on the first floor, and a new master bedroom on the second. Bath and storage spaces have been added on both levels as well. The library hallway runs along one edge of the two lower rooms, proceeding up the curving stairway – which is modelled after a nautilus shell – to the master suite. A glowing lightwell over the staircase draws one up to the second-floor spaces and sheds light on the stairway and bookshelves.

The upper level of the addition was conceived as a total retreat for the Woos, with a beautiful view of the lake and an abundance of natural light. It is the largest space in the house, containing a master bedroom and a studio with a large corner window.

Clad in stucco, the walls of the addition appear to buckle and pull away in places, revealing, and illuminating, an interior world.

Silver Lake, California

PP72-3: Composite plans/sections; P75: Trellis detail;
PP76-7, FROM ABOVE: Second level, first level

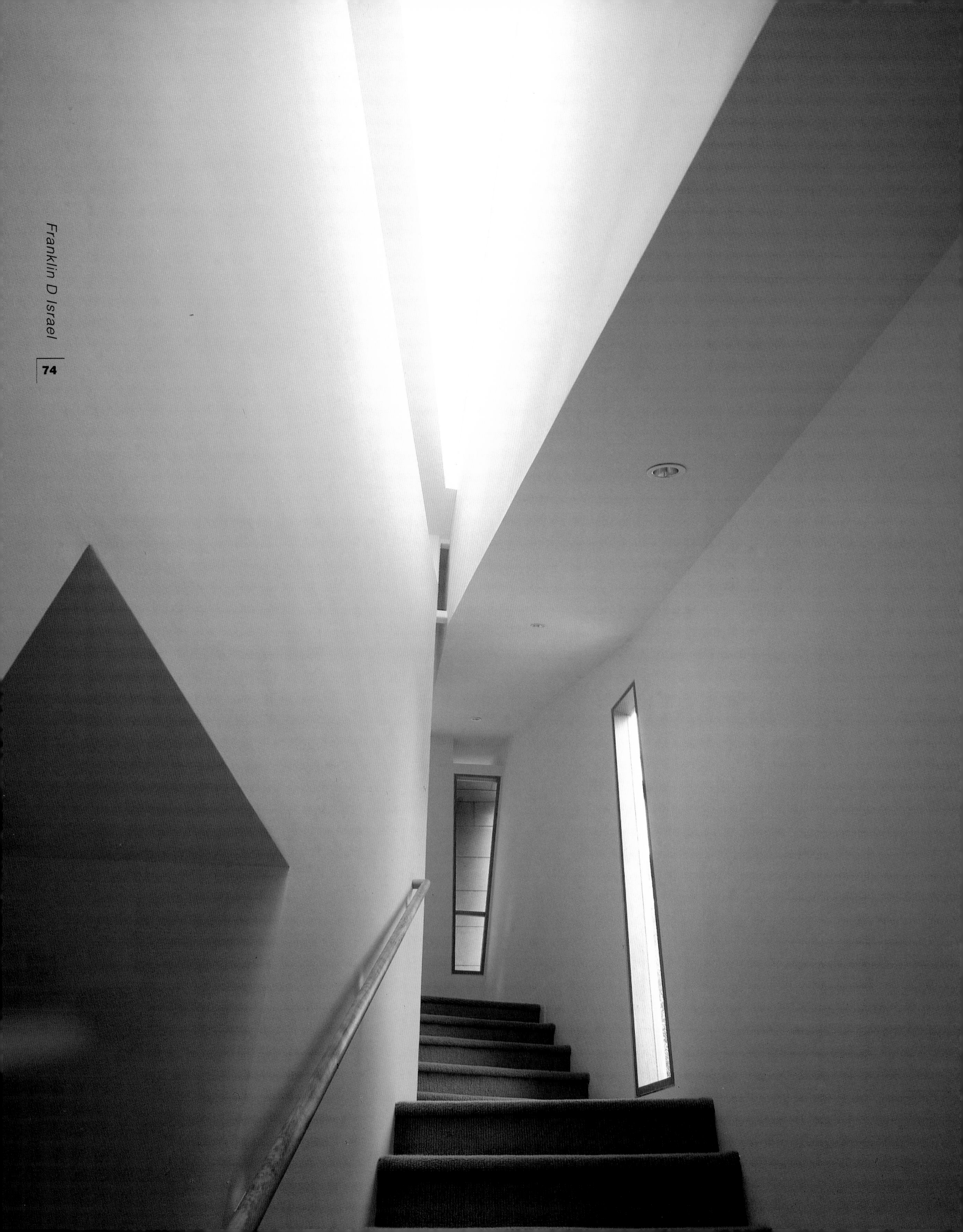

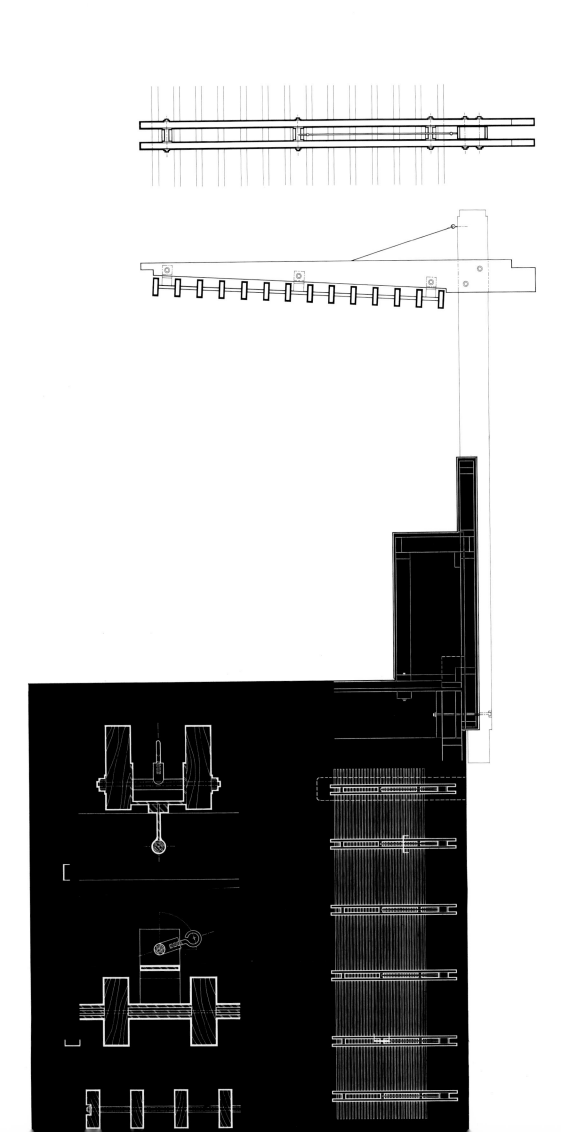

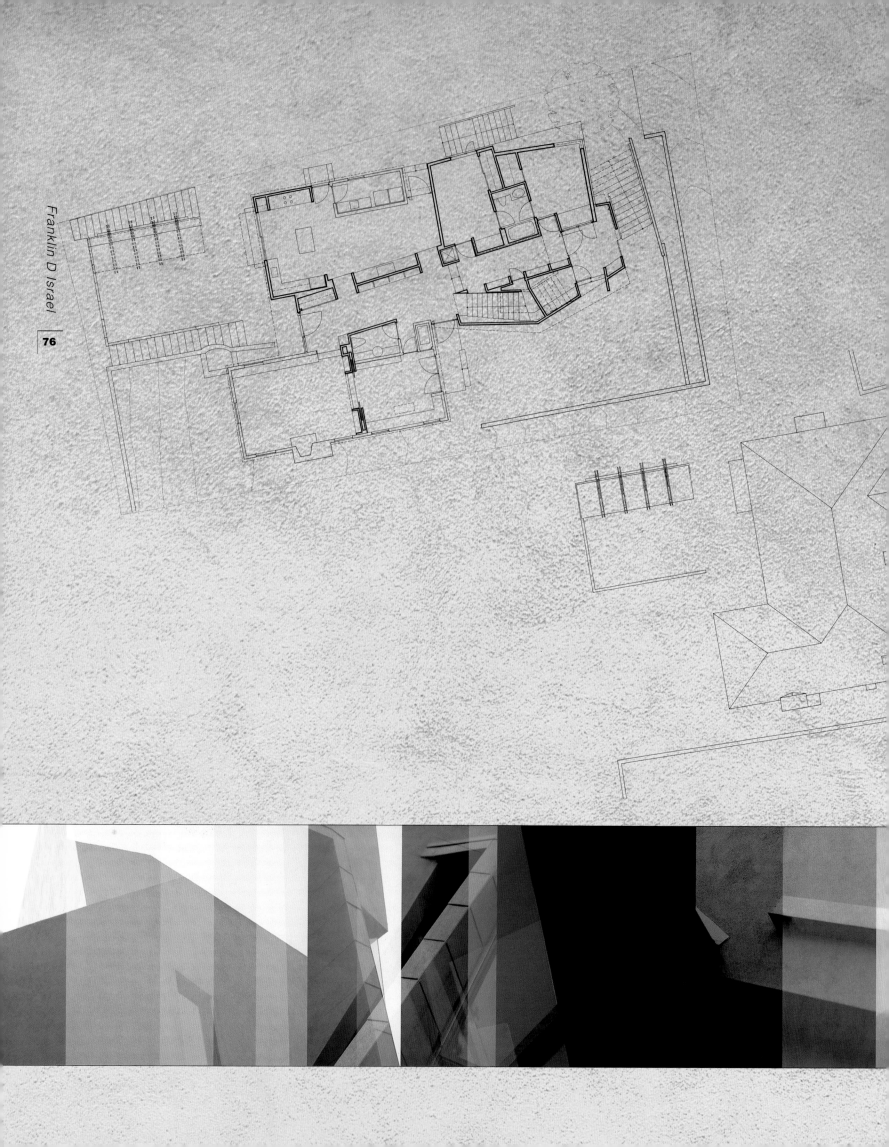

B RIGHT AND ASSOCIATES

1991

The project at 901 W Washington Boulevard in Venice involved the renovation and transformation of a group of three buildings dating from 1929, which had served originally as a train-shed, then as a funeral parlour, and most recently as the offices of Charles and Ray Eames.

The scheme developed from an interest in creating a processional sequence with a beginning, middle, and end. The subconscious influence of the Eames can be seen in certain details.

At the exterior, a steel and glass canopy defines the start of a dramatic entry sequence. The interior entry courtyard is a skylit, two-story space similar to a Tuscan *cortile*, except that here no plane is parallel to another. Once inside, one passes through a tunnel that ends with an inverted cone conference room of birch plywood in the largest and oldest building on the site. One moves along this interior street past the executive design offices, into the large design room, and on into the production area. The axis is terminated by an obelisk marking the photo reproduction area, which is lit from above. The interior atrium is visible as it pops up above the roof.

Outside, various sculptural objects have been placed in strategic relation to the existing structures. Composed of steel, glass, and sheet metal, they link the buildings to its Venice context and mark various crucial pieces of the building – entrance, fire stair, and street address.

The history of the site and the musings of Charles Eames determined a strategy which left much of the exterior unchanged. The eucalyptus trees hark back to the grove at the Eames house in Pacific Palisades. The trees are reflected in the white, concrete block entry – another reminder of Charles Eames, who said that the reflections of natural phenomena are as rich and enduring as a painting.

Venice, California

P82: Floor plan; P83: Cross sections; PP84-5, FROM ABOVE: Exterior isometric, interior isometric; P88: Axonometric of executive office, P93: Preliminary sketches.

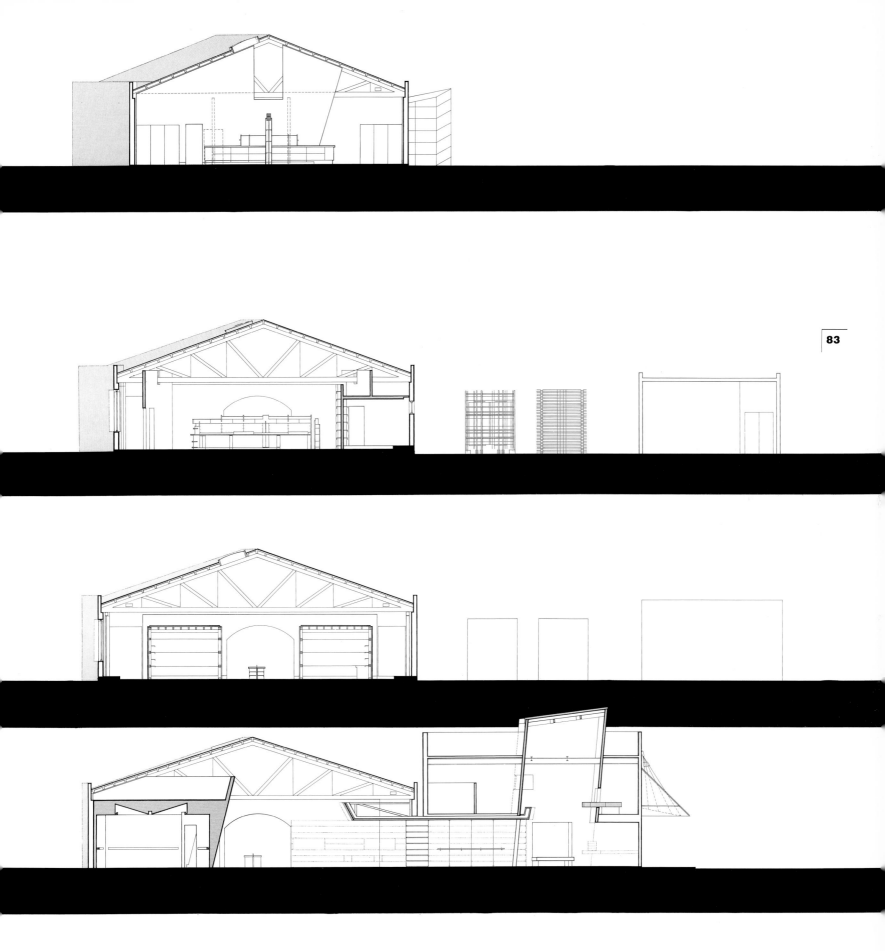

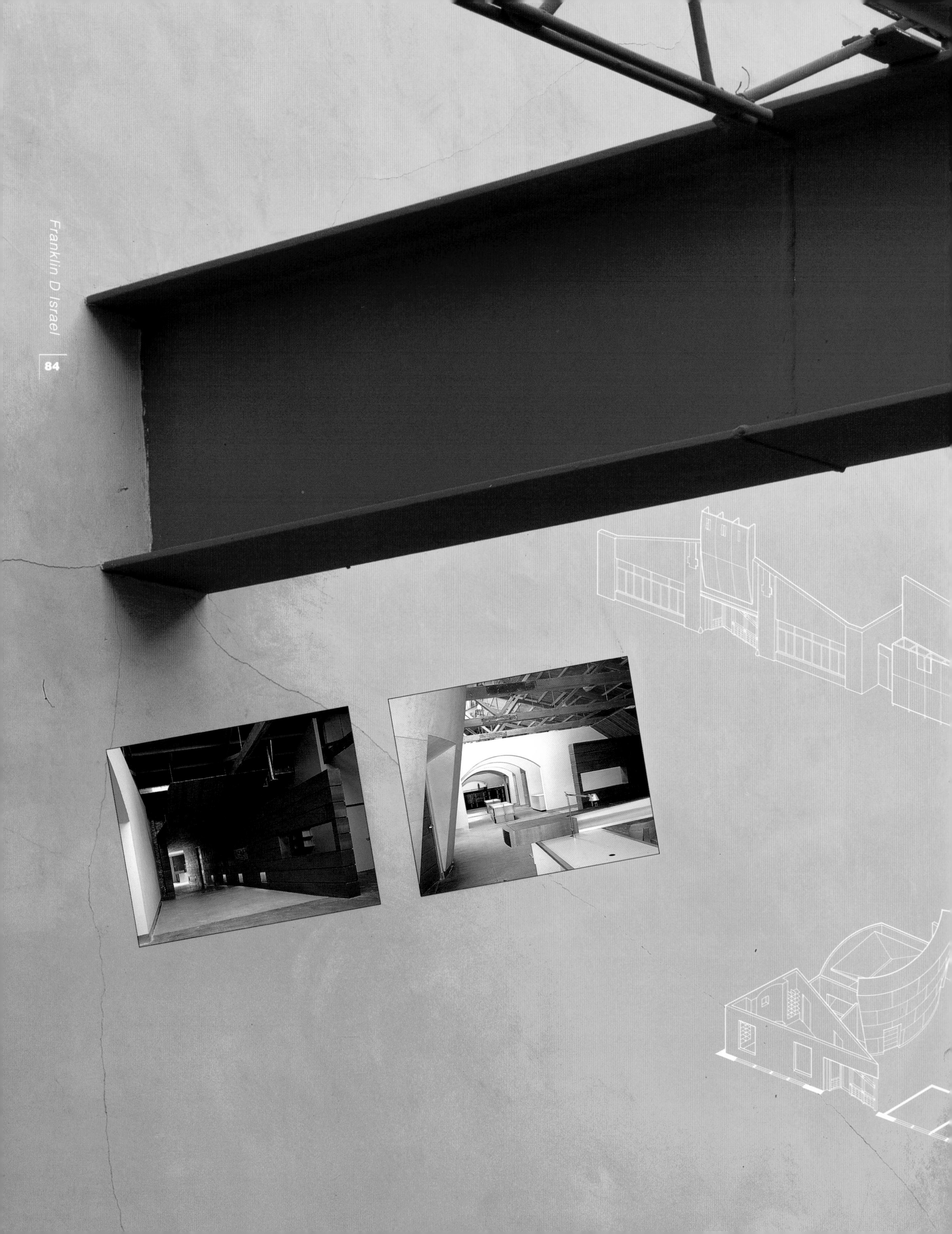

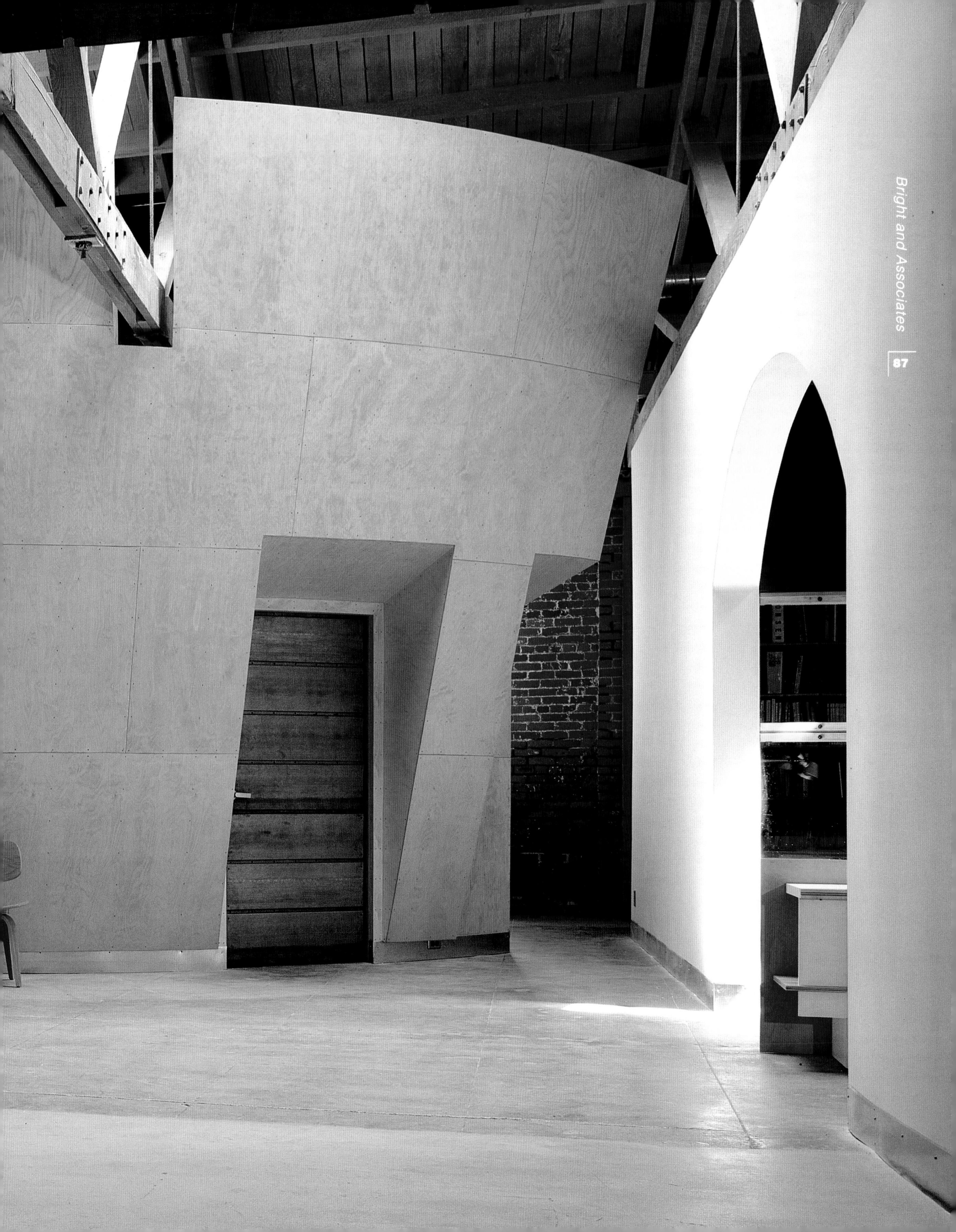

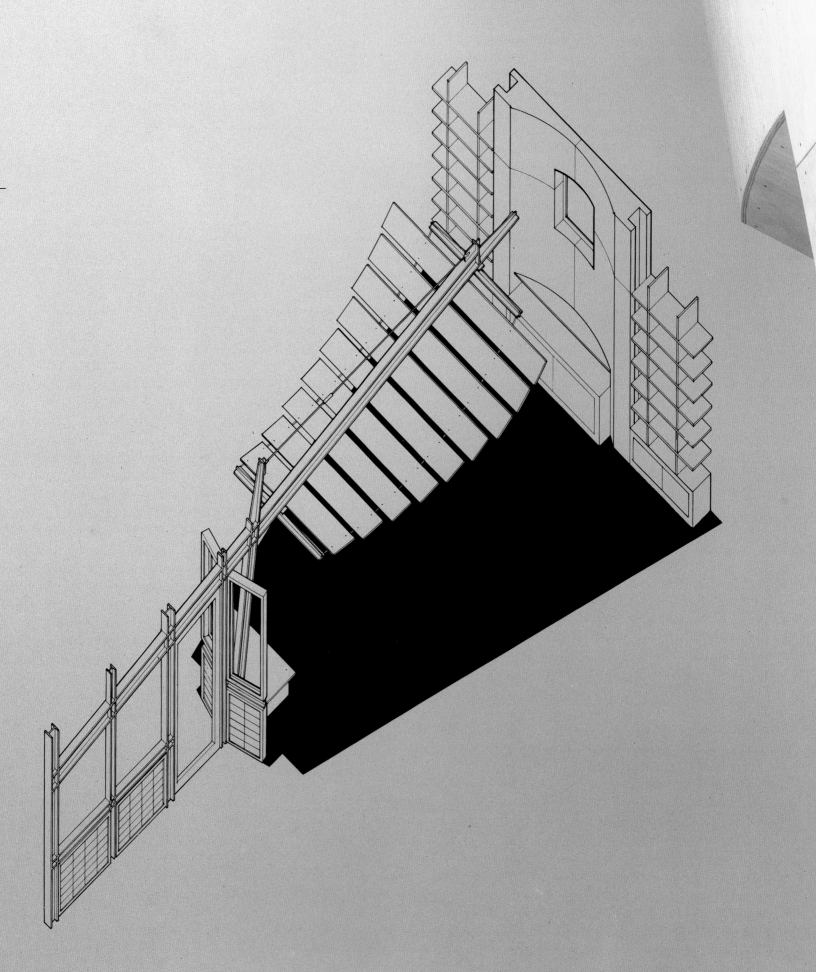

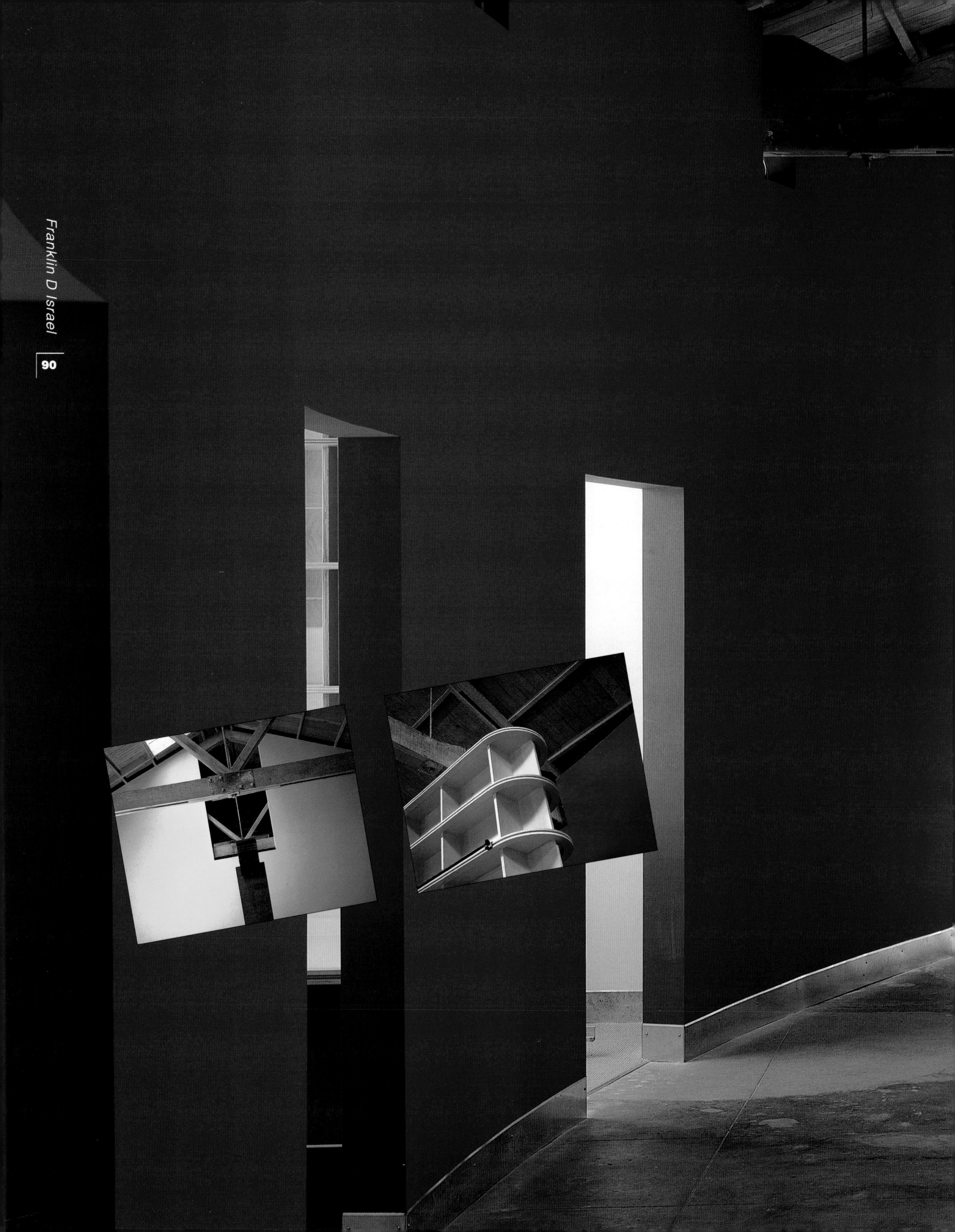

BRIGHT.

level -1

level 3

BUNKA SHUTTER

1992

A city within, and on the edge, this commission is divided into two phases. On a site along the northern perimeter of Tokyo a 'New Industrial City' is proposed, comprising offices, laboratories, and studios for architects, graphic and industrial designers. Central to this plan is the metro station which brings people into a series of public spaces enclosed and defined by galleries, shops, and cafés. Less formal than other urban projects in Tokyo, the 'New Industrial City' borrows the open air logic of the original 'Cité Industrielle' of Tony Garnier, taking advantage of its proximity to a landscaped hillside park and a planted river basin. The design extends these landscaped features into the plan as a series of terraced platforms, which in turn form the base for a series of office blocks along the main vehicular corridor of the site.

The headquarters for Bunka Shutter, a prominent building products company, crowns the design. The semi-transparent tower sits on a garden platform that includes studios, laboratories, and other facilities. Bunka Shutter products are used in facade and plan to transform the tower into a catalogue 'billboard'. These components – windows, shutters, and overhead doors – highlight the design and affirm the graceful precision of the company and its products. They create a kinetic building which changes according to the location of the sun at different times of the day and year.

Tokyo, Japan

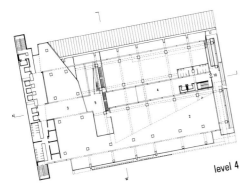

level 4

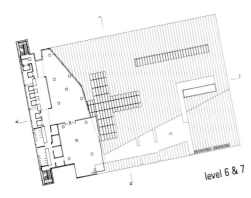

level 6 & 7

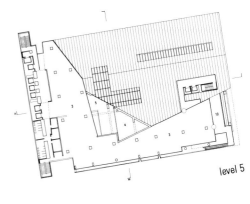

level 5

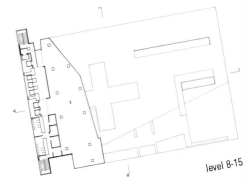

level 8-15

LEFT: First and third levels; FROM ABOVE L TO R: Levels four, five, six to seven and eight to fifteen; PP96-97: Headquarters; P98: Cross section through scheme; P99: Side elevation of the Bunka Shutter building

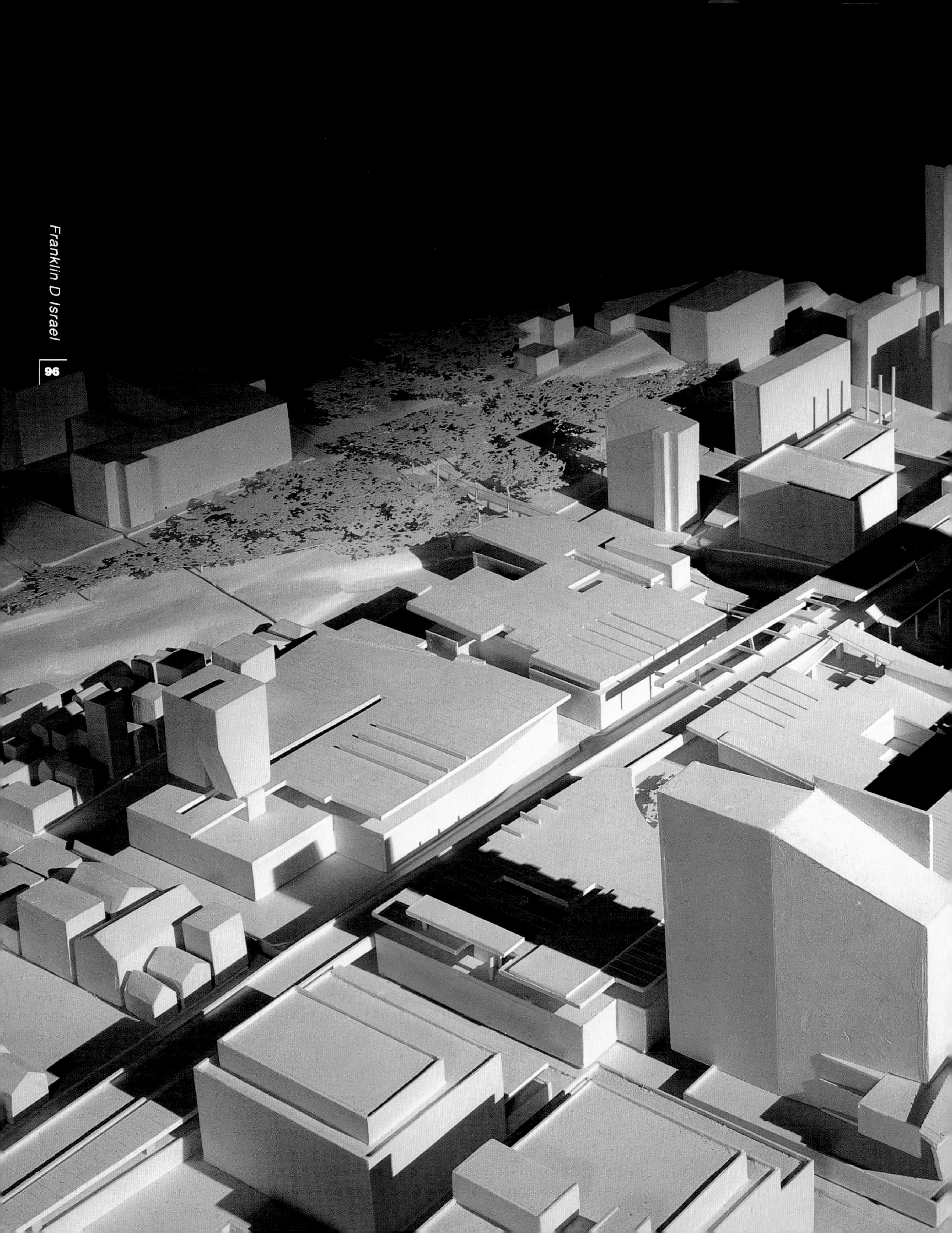

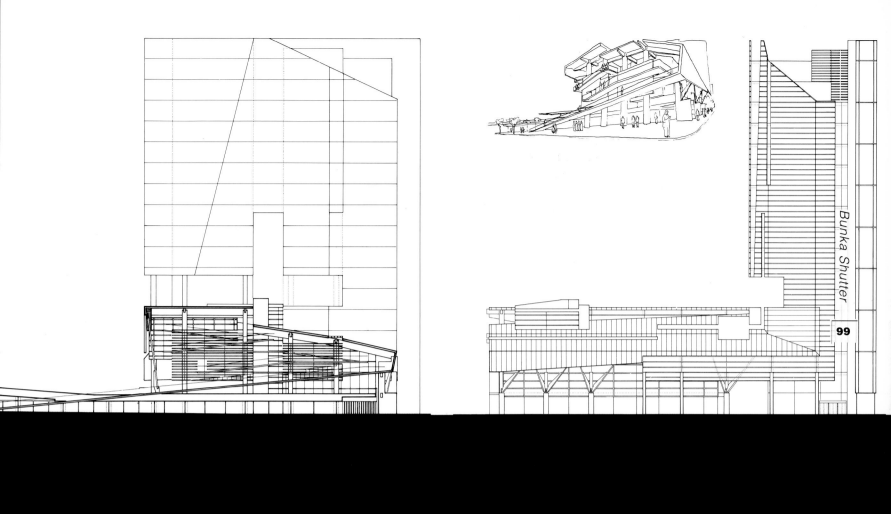

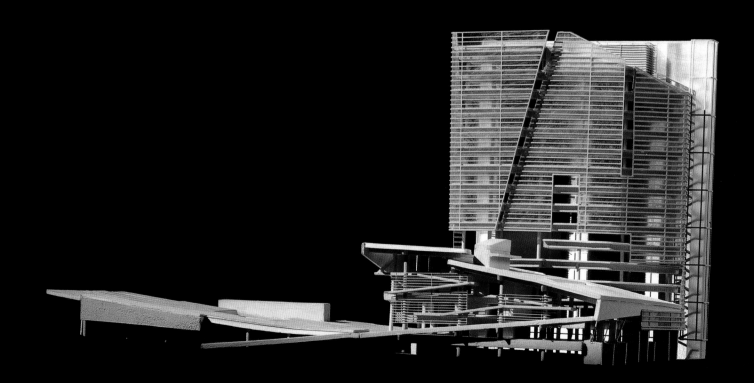

LIMELIGHT PRODUCTIONS

1991

The Limelight Productions project has been dubbed 'Day for Night', appropriating a film aphorism which describes a situation where a night-time shooting is floodlit to represent day. In movie production, it is not unusual to work around the clock and several days running. Because of these long hours, the interior of the building needed to function like an urban village. Working with an existing large double-bay warehouse space in Hollywood, Day for Night was achieved with a series of backlit fibreglass panels and three large diagonal piers tied to a celestial soffit.

Much of the design focused on the careful articulation of a spatial sequence beginning outside the western wall and continuing through the entire length of the interior. A canopied entrance leads to a large workroom akin to the one in Wright's Johnson Wax Building. Colour and materials accentuate sculptural elements symbolising a new administrative network for the company – major executive offices, electronic information centres, and points of communication.

Employing another illusionistic film device, conference rooms and public spaces were concentrated near the entrance so that the visitor would perceive a complex far larger than reality.

A consistent logic was applied to materials, details, and colour scheme. Aluminum elements – fasteners, joints, and sheeting – serve as structural supports and as the only embellishments to birch plywood cabinetry and utilitarian office interiors. Glass and fibreglass provide a light-transforming counterbalance to the otherwise opaque composition, in recognition of the foremost requirement of film-viewing: light passing through celluloid.

Los Angeles, California

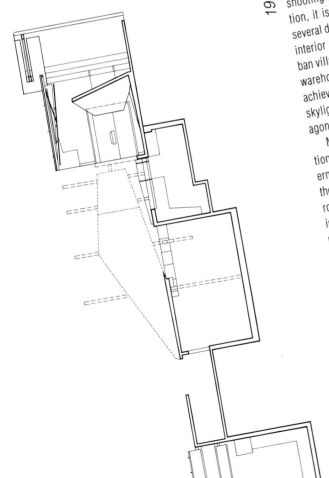

ABOVE LEFT: Sectional elevation and plan of entry sequence; PP102-3: Ground plan, section axonometric; P106: Section, elevation, and plan of lightwall; P107: Entrance plan and axonometric; P109, FROM ABOVE: Section/elevation of entrance, longitudinal section; P111: work-station details

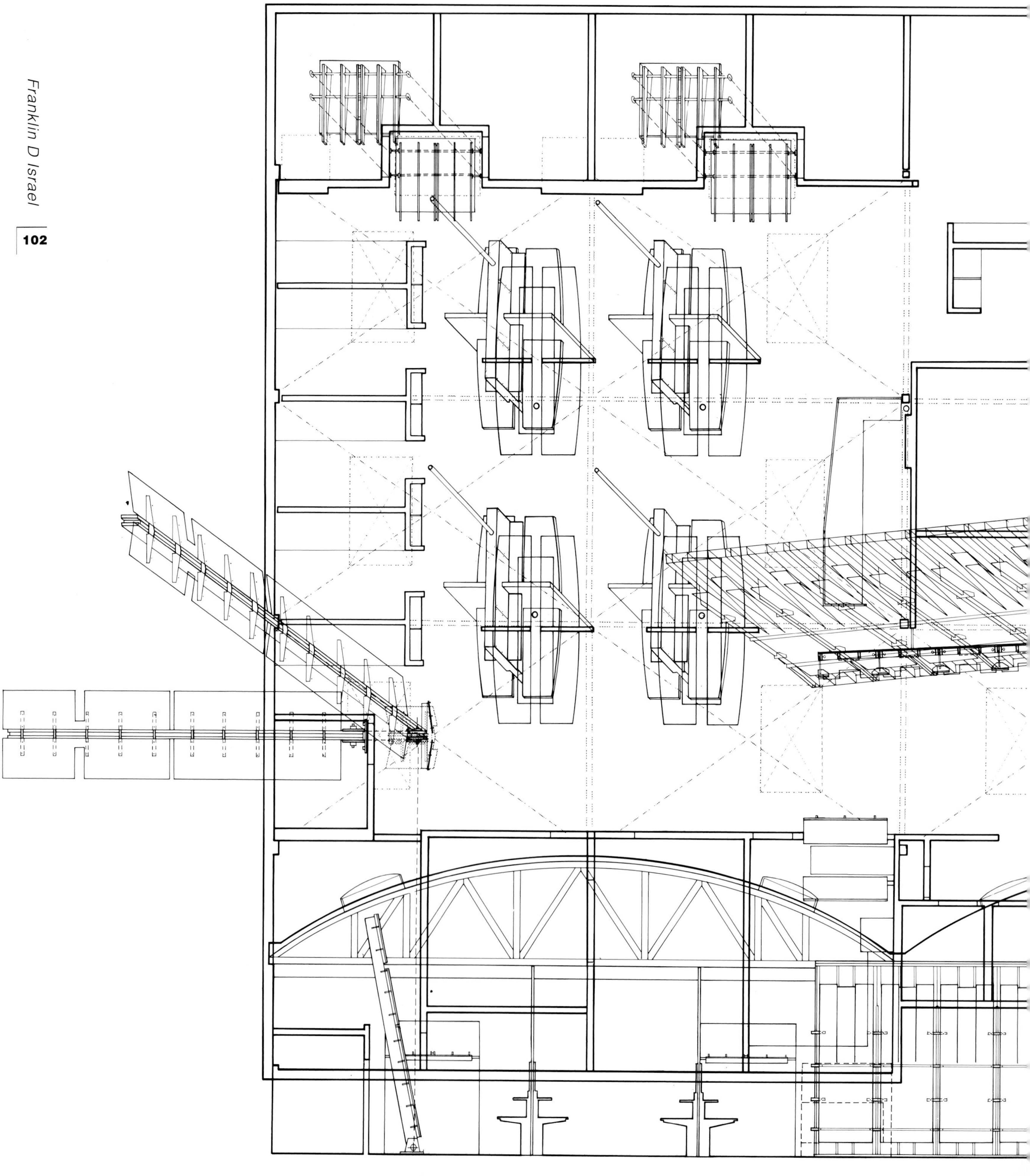

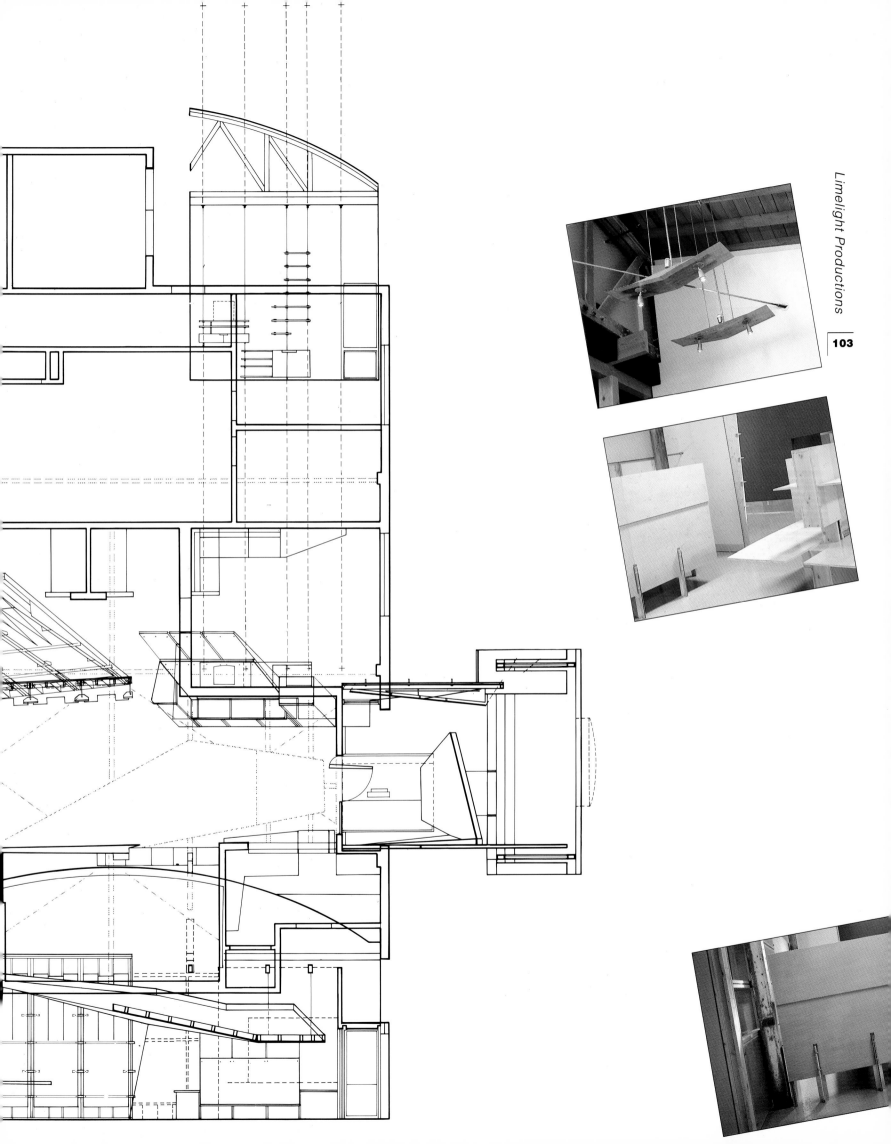

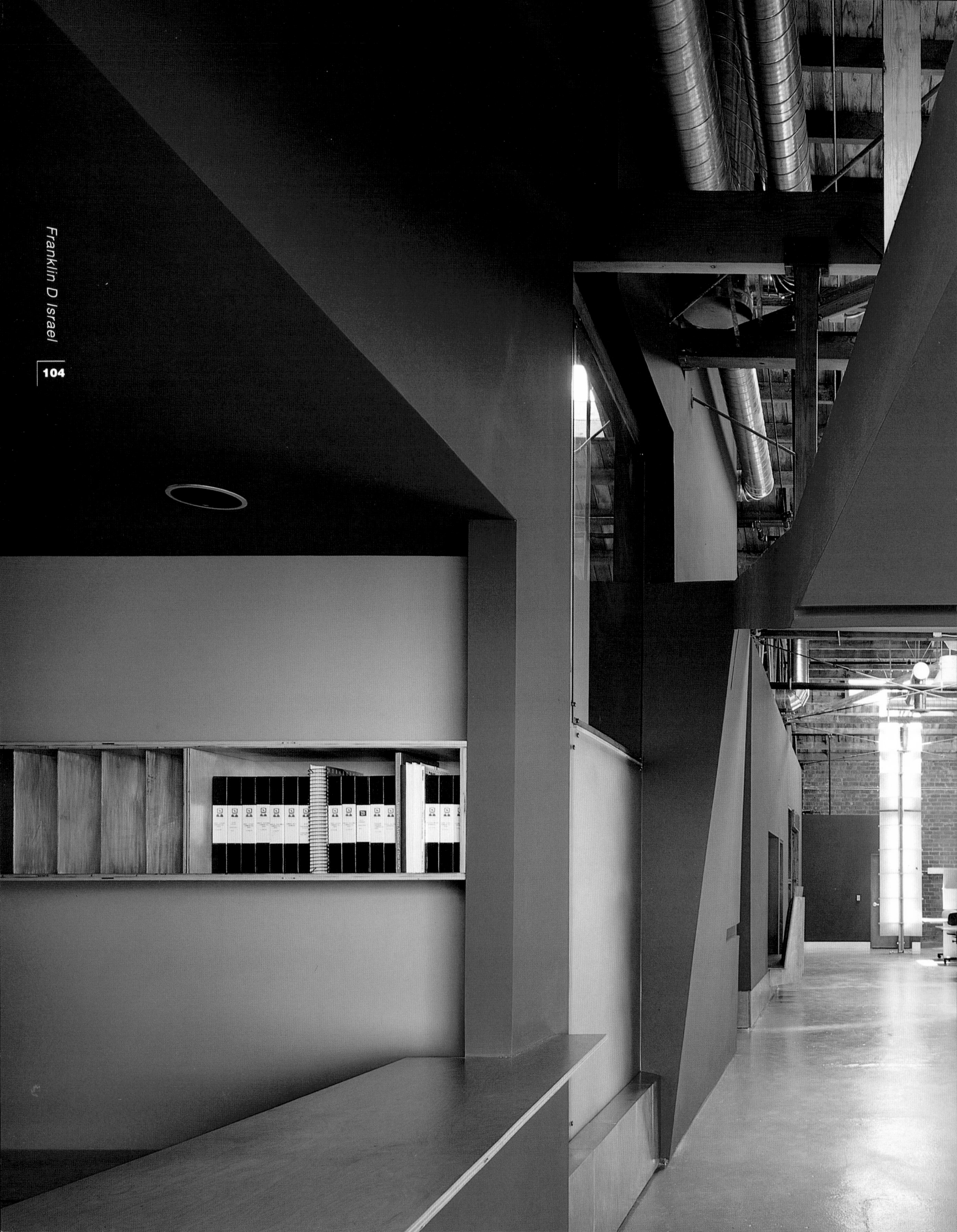

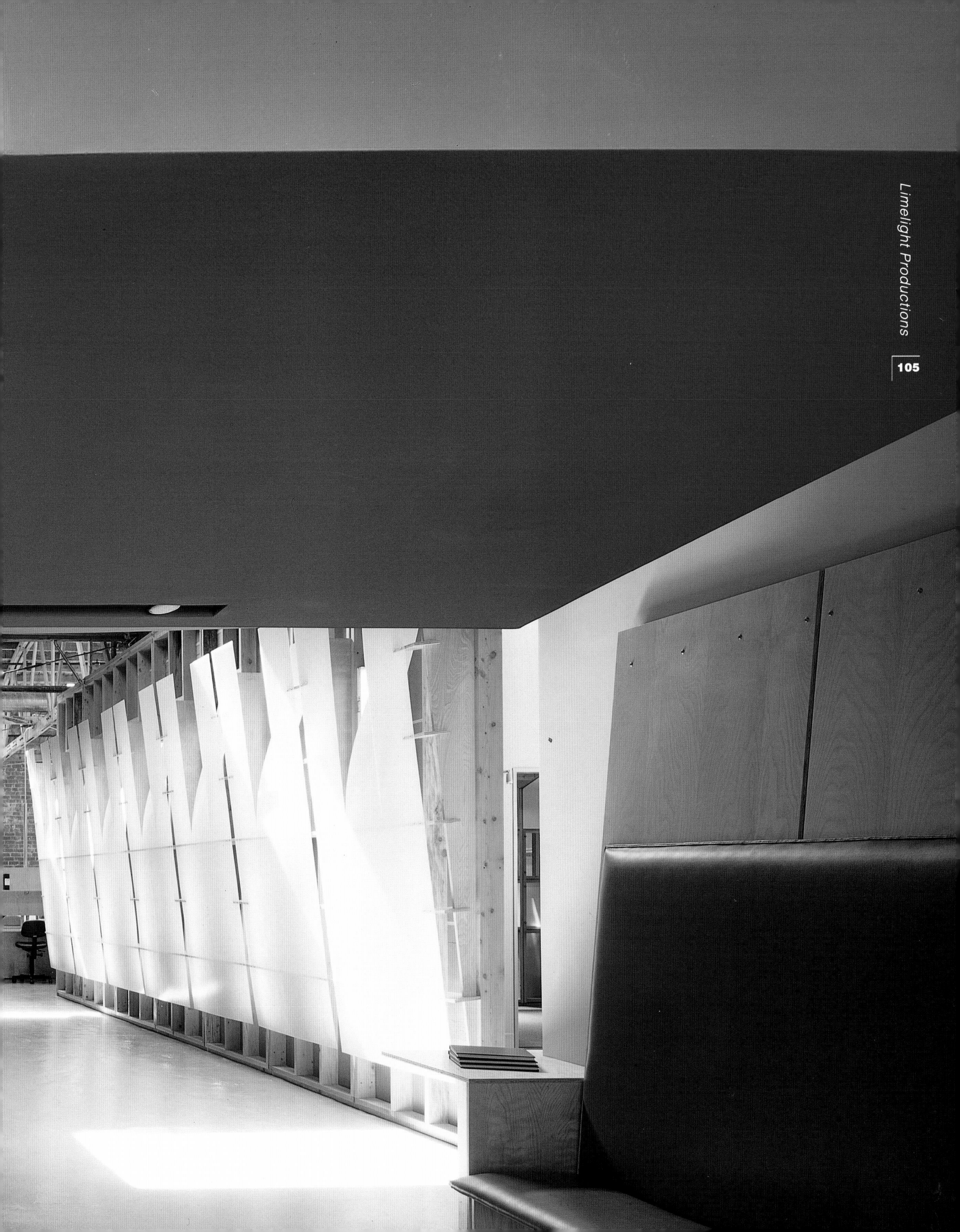

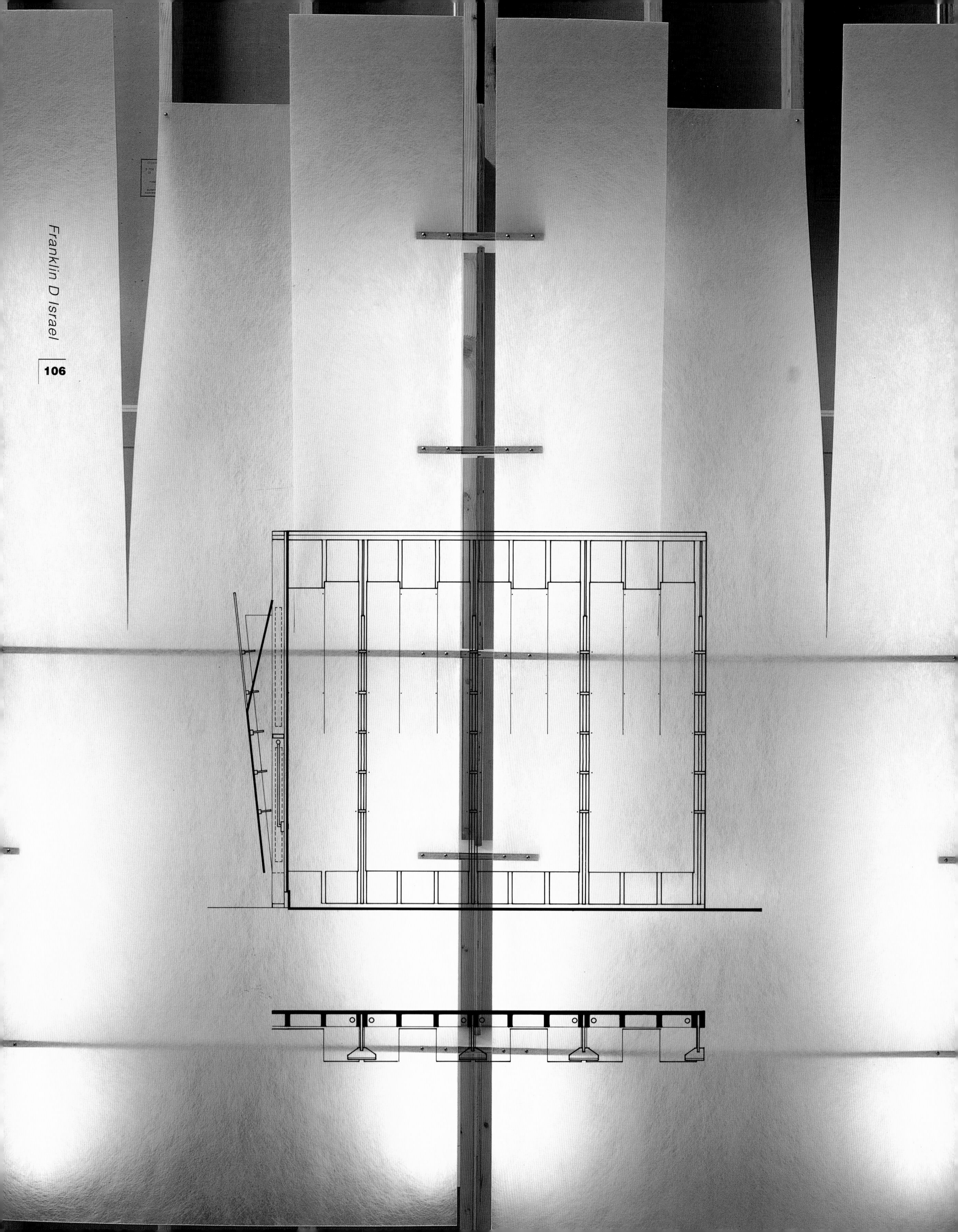

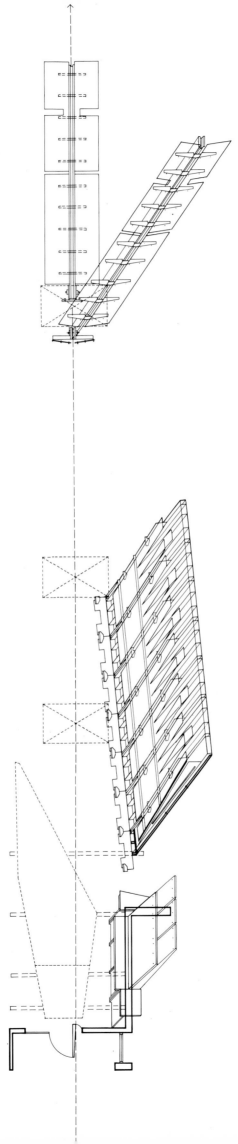

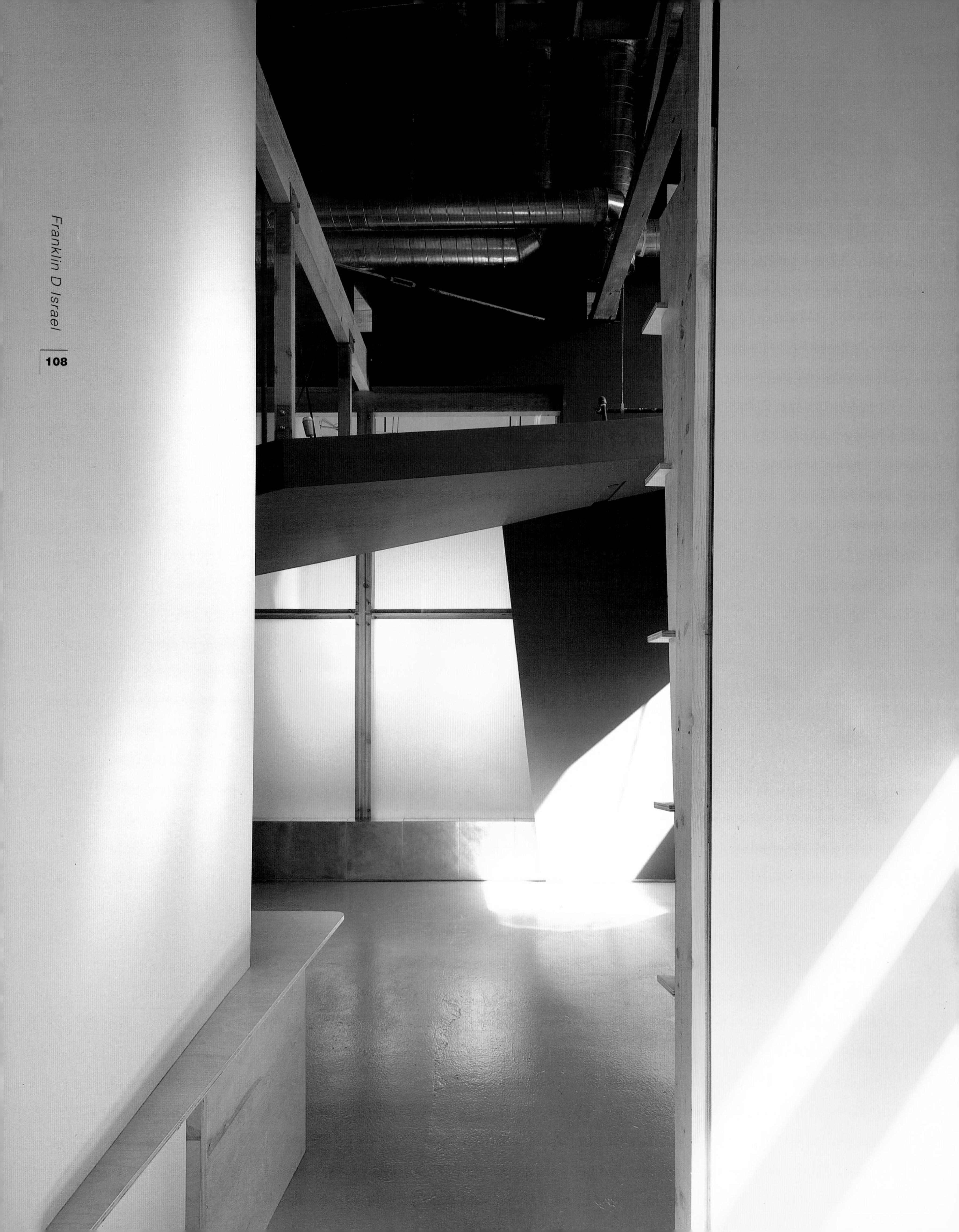

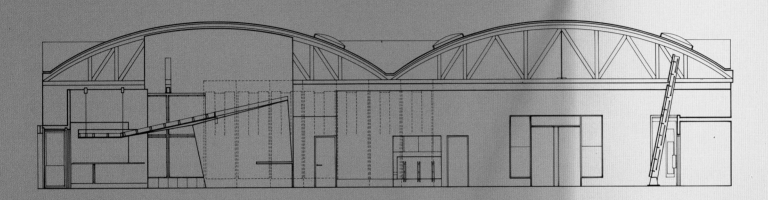

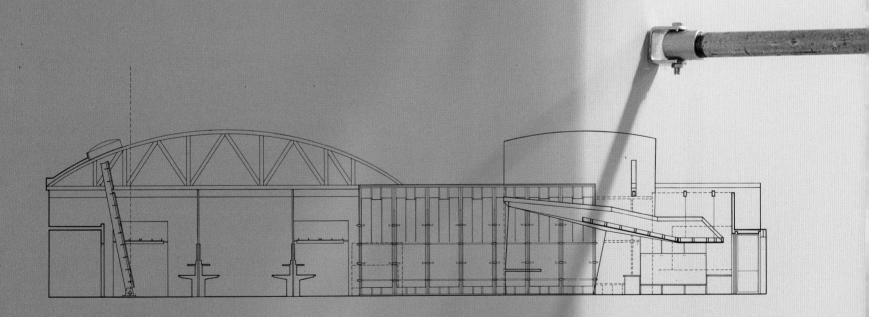

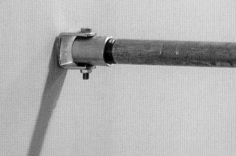

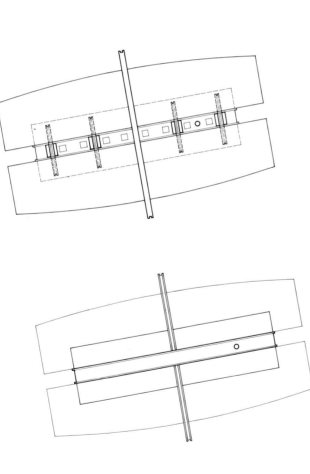

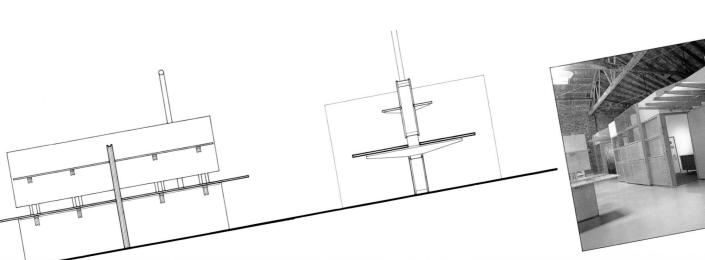

PROMPT EXHIBIT

1993

Making use of the communications highway, this exhibit was designed with the use of the fax machine and telephone.

Critical words were extracted from a larger text and used to generate a cacophony of ideas, from which a scheme was developed. Collaboration between Princeton architecture students and the practice formed a solution based on the exigencies of the situation.

Demonstrating a collection of ideas about frontality, transparency, and materiality, this project reassembled existing exhibit materials and reformed fresh architectural energy.

Princeton, New Jersey

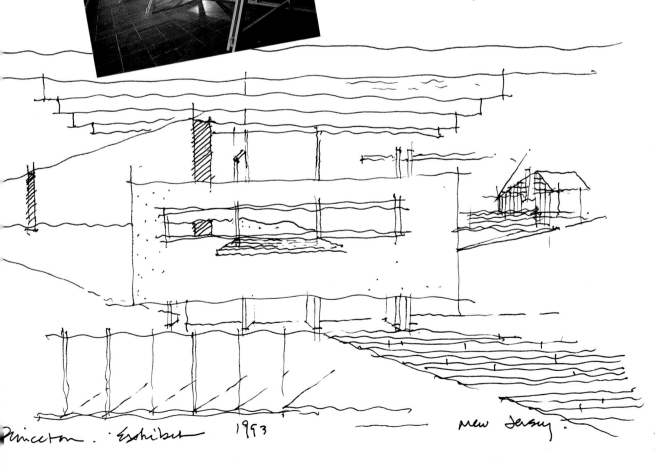

Princeton . Exhibit   1993   new Jersey.

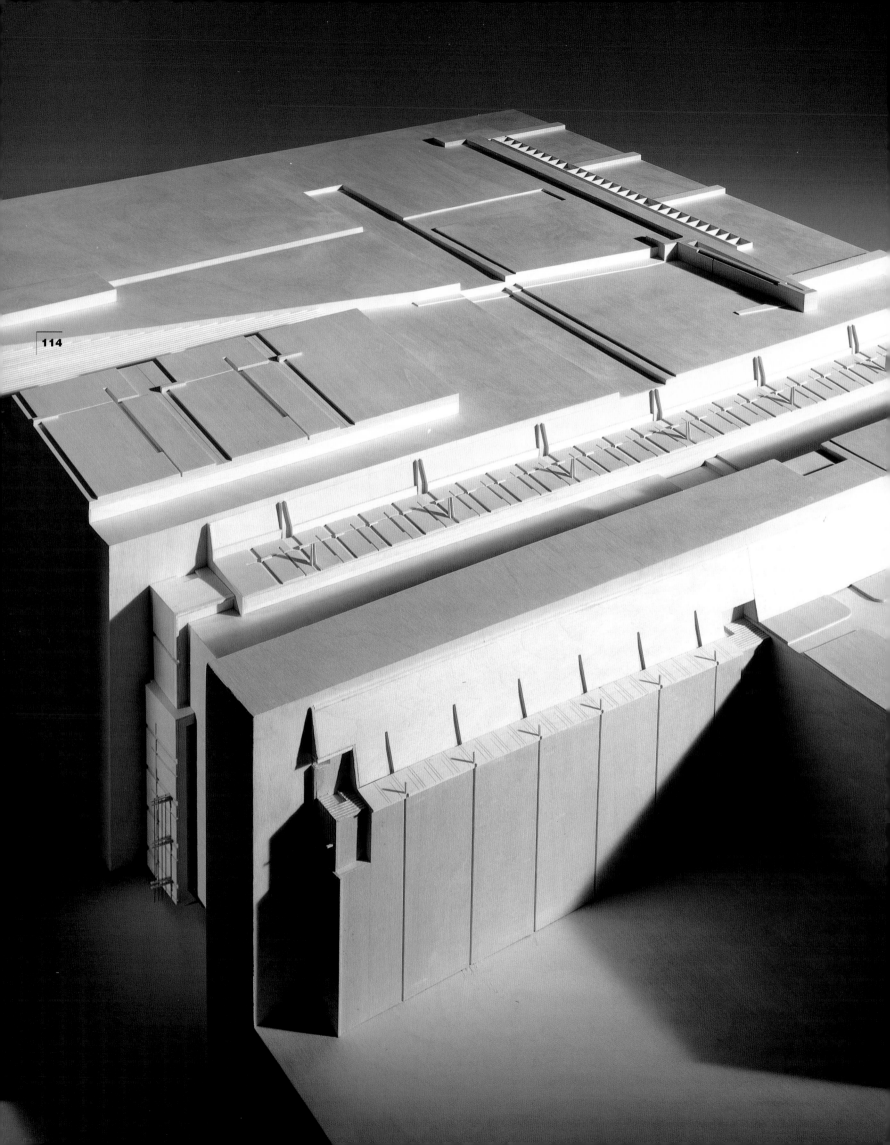

U CLA SRL

1991

The addition to the existing Southern Regional Library is no conventional building because the site is mainly underground, forming a giant earth berm. What is seen is a series of concrete panels linked vertically to form a visual plinth to the original building. These panels are interrupted by a series of steel troughs forming scuppers to receive water collected from the roof. The scuppers are on axis with slots in the earth berm which carry water to the storm drains at street grade.

Celebrating building as landscape, the new addition promises to form a clear and coherent western edge to the UCLA campus. At the same time, its discrete presence in relation to its residential neighbours improves the landscape of the area as a whole.

Brick is the material of linkage. It complements the more formal buildings of center campus and articulates the joints between the original library and the almost obscured addition, yet it also outlines the edges of the site.

Westwood, California

ABOVE: Site plan; BELOW: Isometric perspective; P116: Composite plan/elevation/section; P117, FROM ABOVE: Front elevation, side elevation; P118: Construction detail

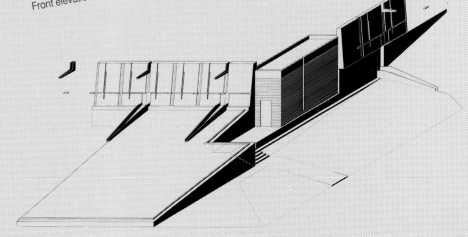

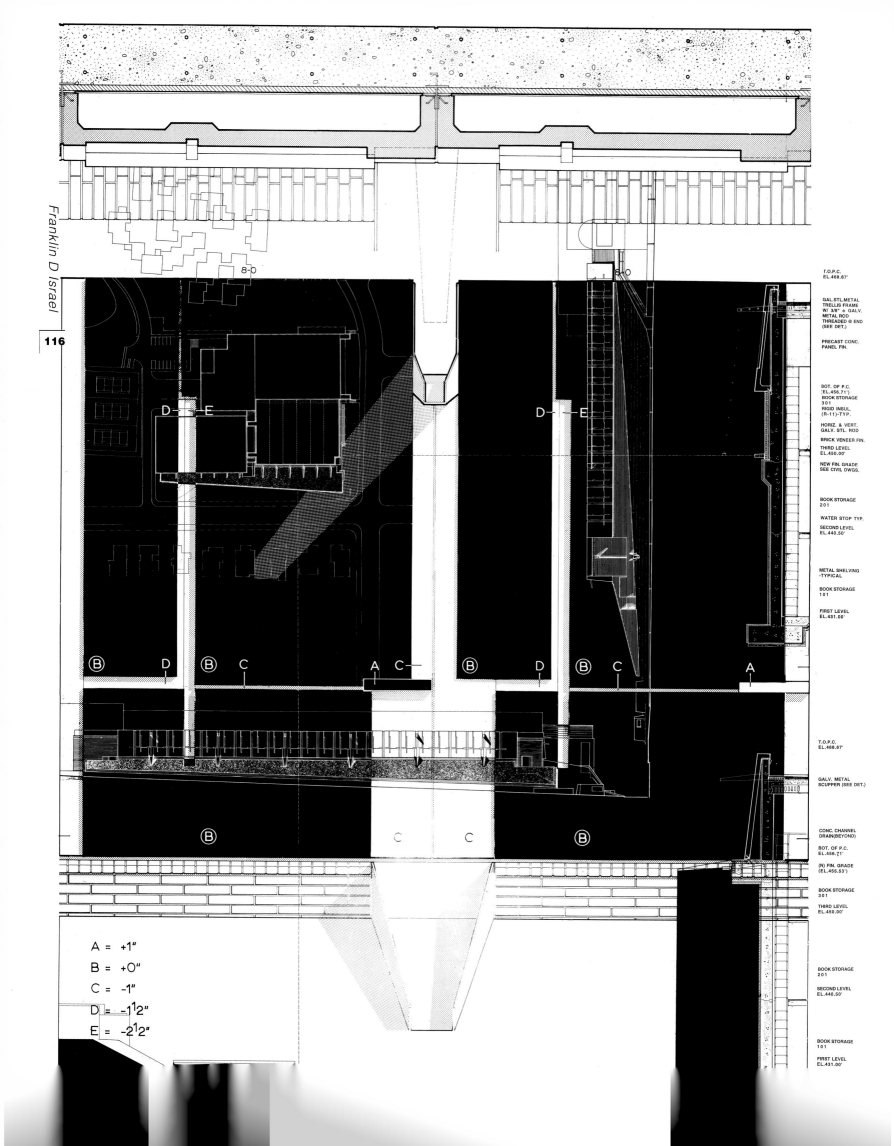

T.O.P.C.
EL.468.67'

GAL.STL.METAL
TRELLIS FRAME
W/ 3/8" ⌀ GALV.
METAL ROD
THREADED @ END
(SEE DET.)

PRECAST CONC.
PANEL FIN.

BOT. OF P.C.
(EL.456.71')
BOOK STORAGE
301
RIGID INSUL.
(R-11)-TYP.

HORIZ. & VERT.
GALV. STL. ROD

BRICK VENEER FIN.

THIRD LEVEL
EL.450.00'

NEW FIN. GRADE
SEE CIVIL DWGS.

BOOK STORAGE
201

WATER STOP TYP.

SECOND LEVEL
EL.440.50'

METAL SHELVING
-TYPICAL

BOOK STORAGE
101

FIRST LEVEL
EL.431.00'

T.O.P.C.
EL.468.67'

GALV. METAL
SCUPPER (SEE DET.)

CONC. CHANNEL
DRAIN(BEYOND)

BOT. OF P.C.
EL.456.71'

(N) FIN. GRADE
(EL.455.53')

BOOK STORAGE
301

THIRD LEVEL
EL.450.00'

BOOK STORAGE
201

SECOND LEVEL
EL.440.50'

BOOK STORAGE
101

FIRST LEVEL
EL.431.00'

A = +1"

B = +0"

C = -1"

D = -1¹2"

E = -2¹2"

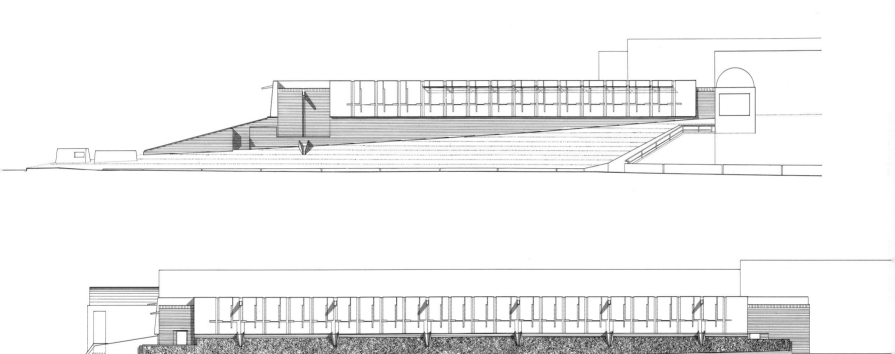

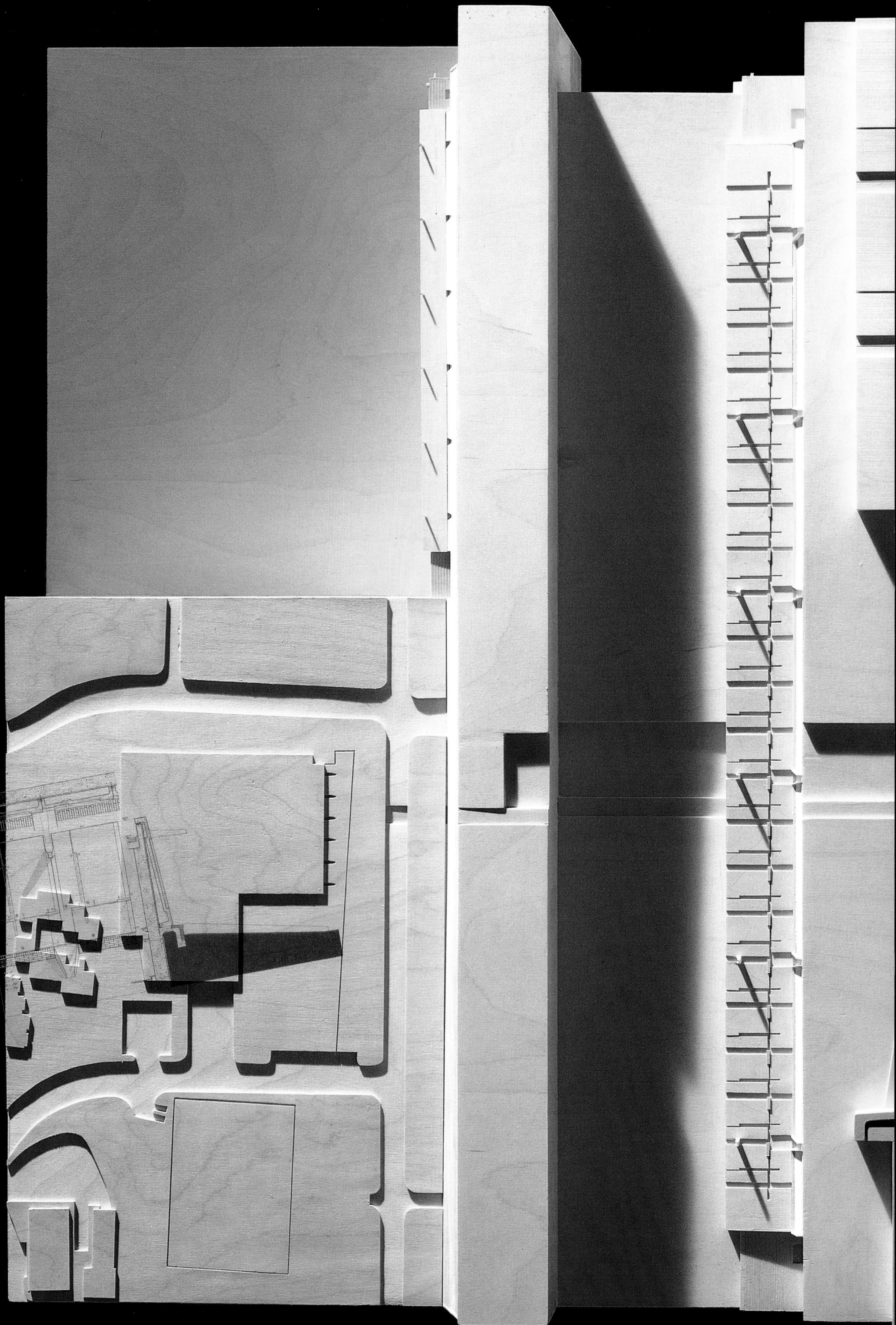

VIRGIN RECORDS

1991

The offices of Virgin Records have assumed a number of forms. The initial project was to be located next to Chiat-Day in Venice. The final site is in Beverly Hills. Requiring the interior and exterior remodelling of a 28,000-square-foot warehouse, this is the largest of the practice's office refurbishment projects.

Because of its widely diversified interests, Virgin required a greater subdivision of office space than usually considered. A corporate division between the business and creative offices led to a near-symmetrical split in the plan of the interior. In this scheme a tighter axial development was opted for than at Bright and Associates or Propaganda Films. Most of the paths were lined with private offices. The grid of closed spaces came to serve as a datum defining the 'negative' space of a T-shaped pathway.

At the intersection of the 'T', a solid cylindrical amphitheatre presents a third zone of space within the interior. As the paths were carved from the office grid, the stairs and stepped seating of the amphitheatre were conceived in the same manner of reductive sculpting: they appear to be cut from a solid round of material, incising alternately for seating and movement.

Following the earlier designs for the Venice site, the exterior plays subtly on the name and nature of Virgin. A low 'V' marks the entrance to the headquarters, and a long, curving outer wall presses out towards the street. The billowing curve recalls the 'hulls' in Israel's previous work and suggests coyly that Virgin may be more pregnant with inspiration than the name would indicate. No longer affronted by the multivalent architectural machismo of the site on main street in Venice, the Virgin complex in Beverly Hills fends off the cool advances of its neighbours with graceful composure.

Beverly Hills, California

P122: Plan, section, and elevation of entrance canopy and wall; P125: Site plan; PP130-1: Sketch of Virgin as fastbowl; P133: Interior elevations and sections

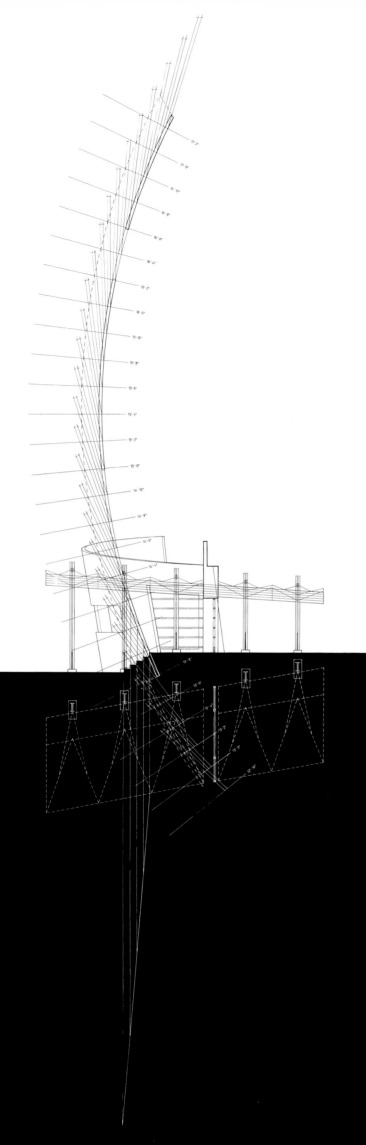

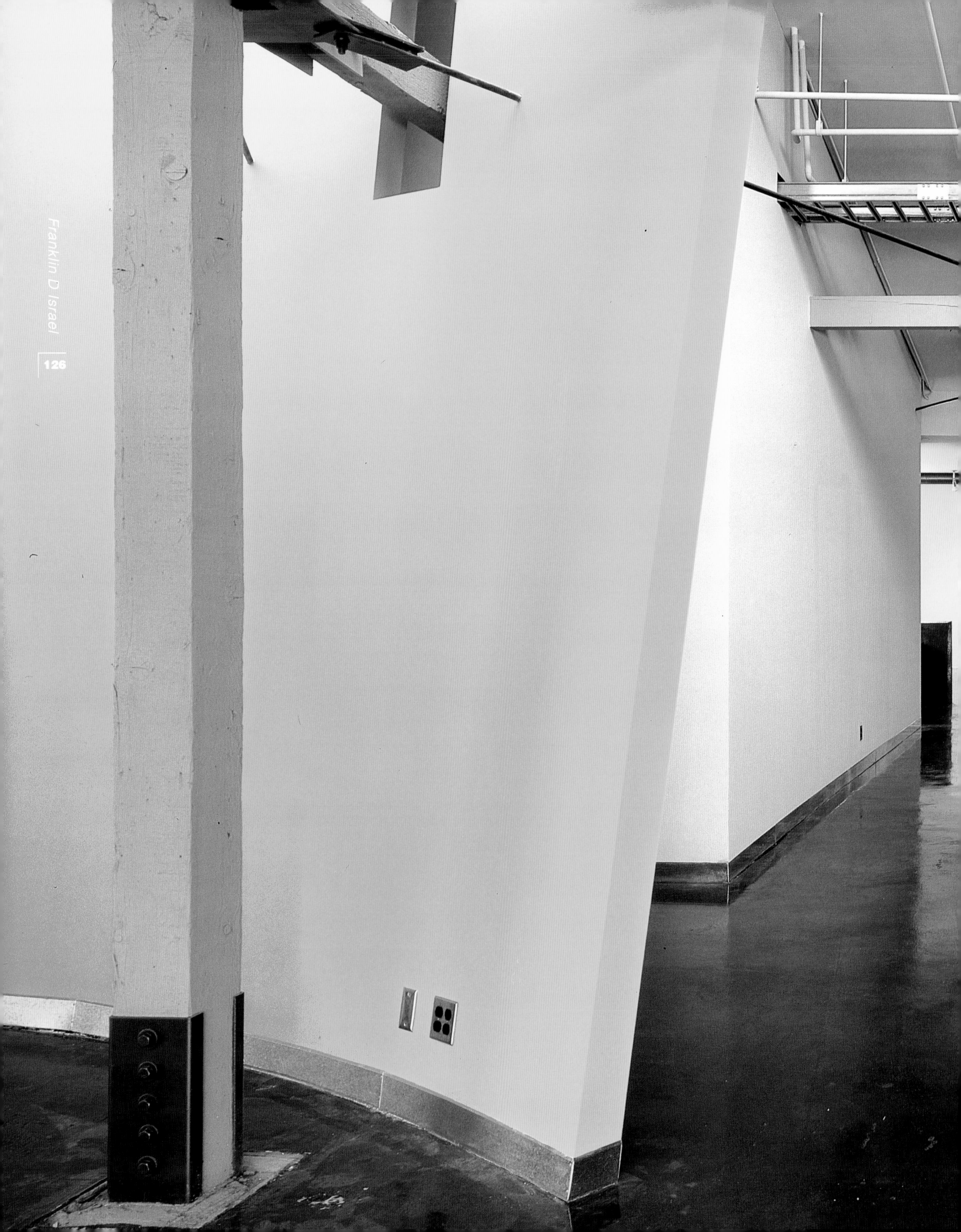

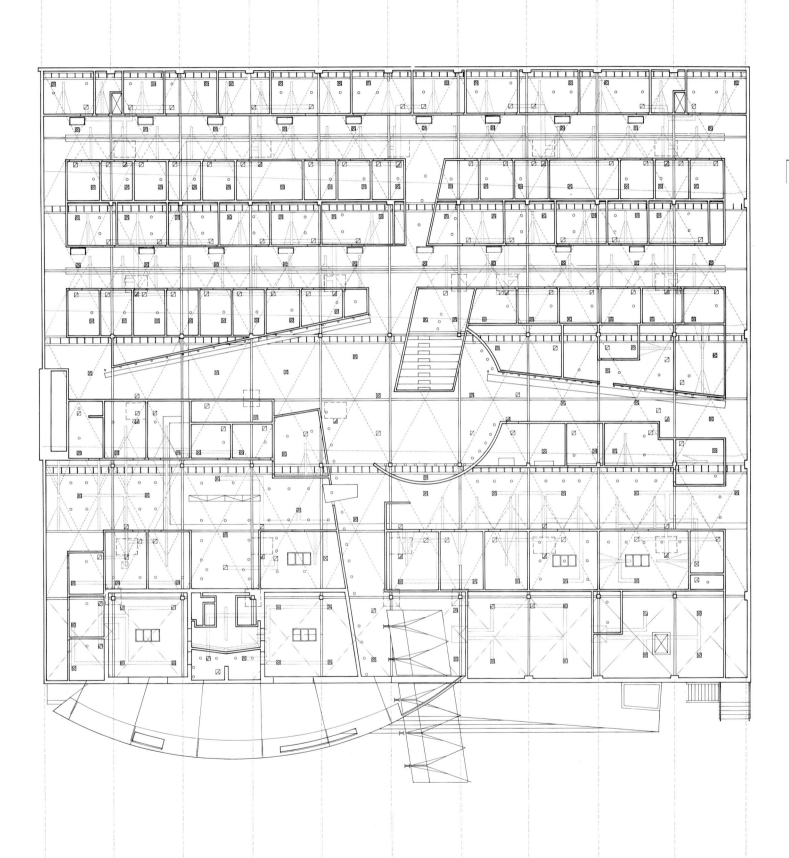

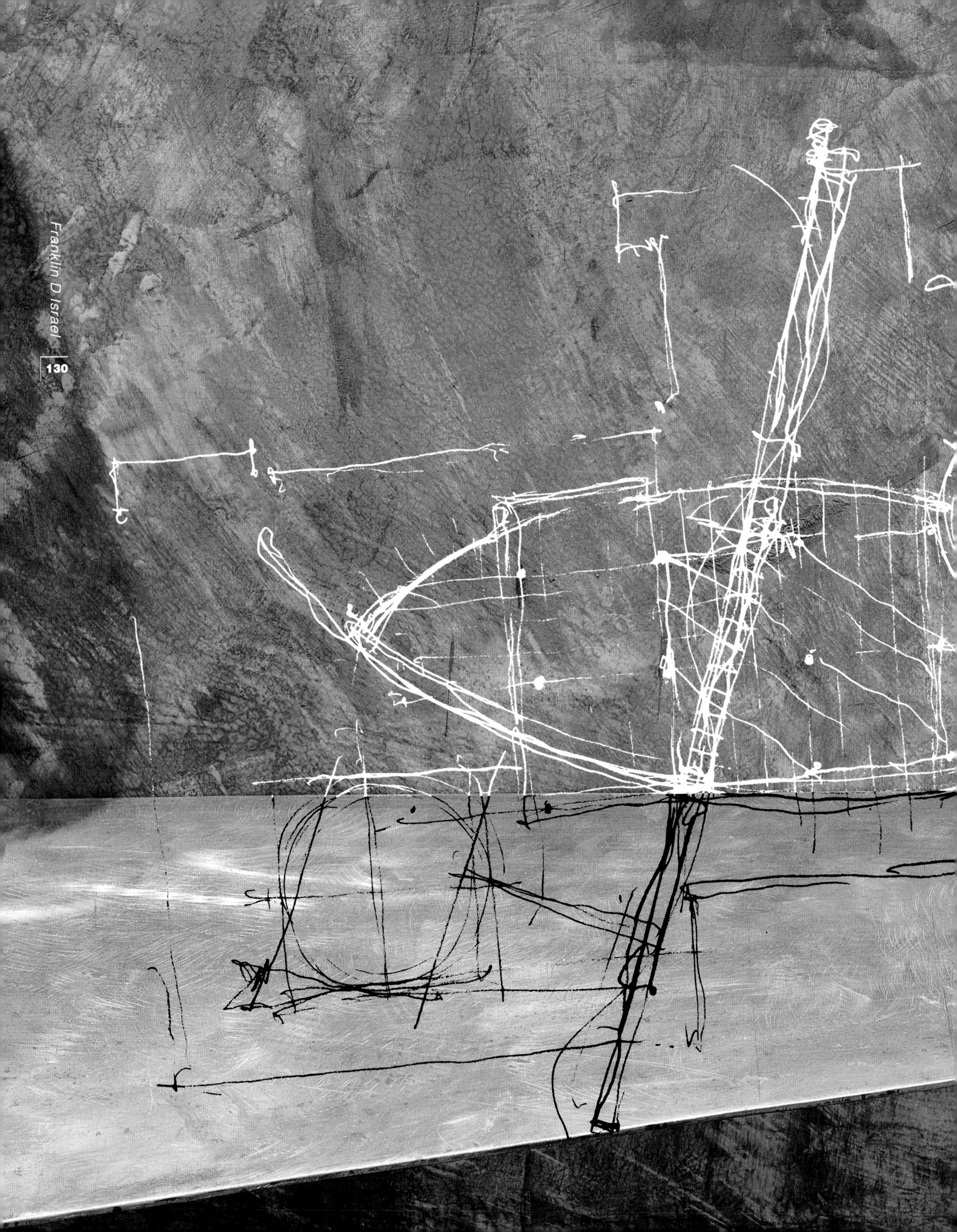

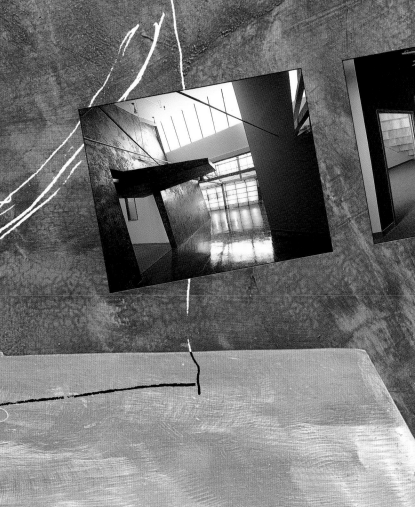

virgin as toothbowl.

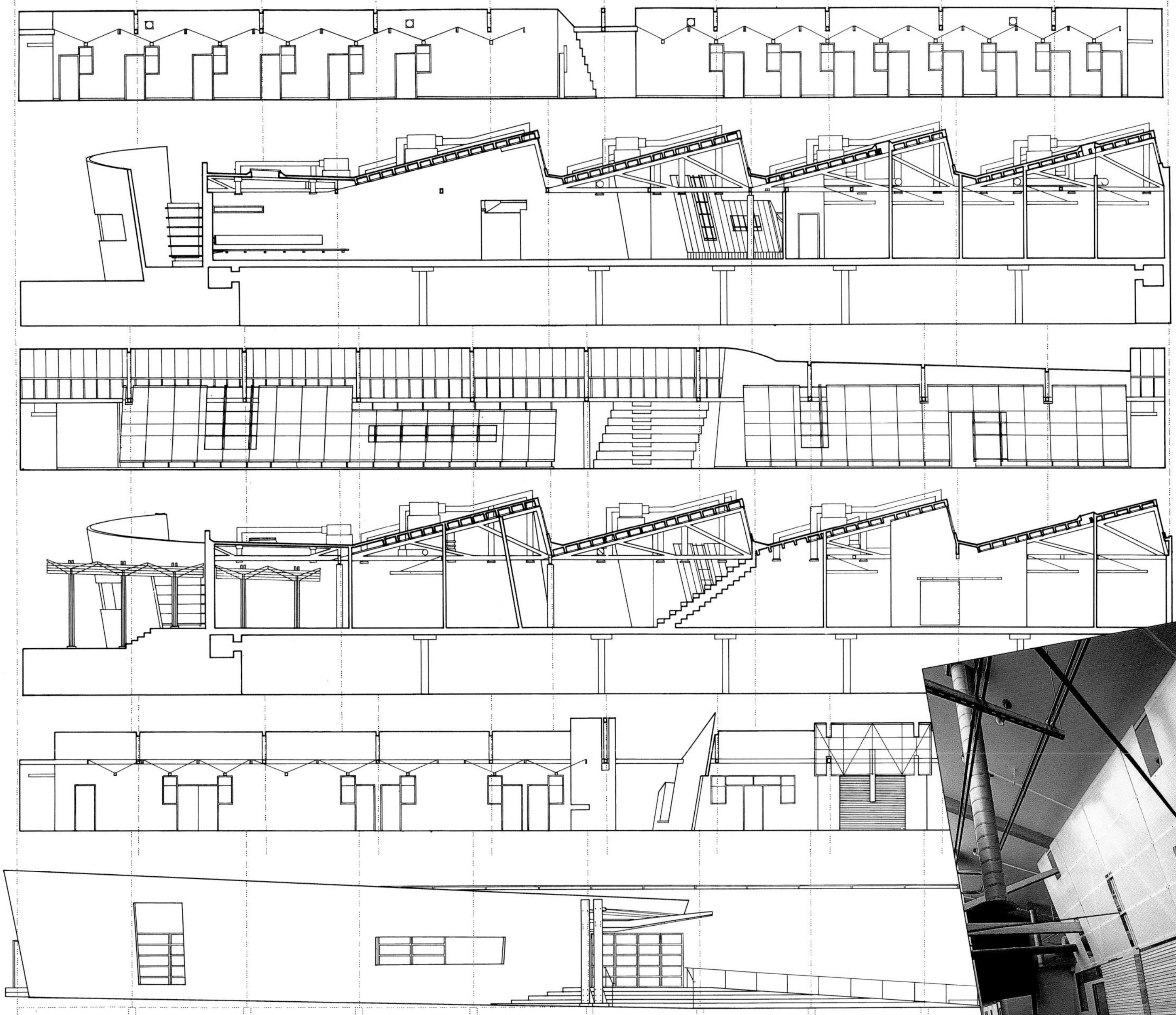

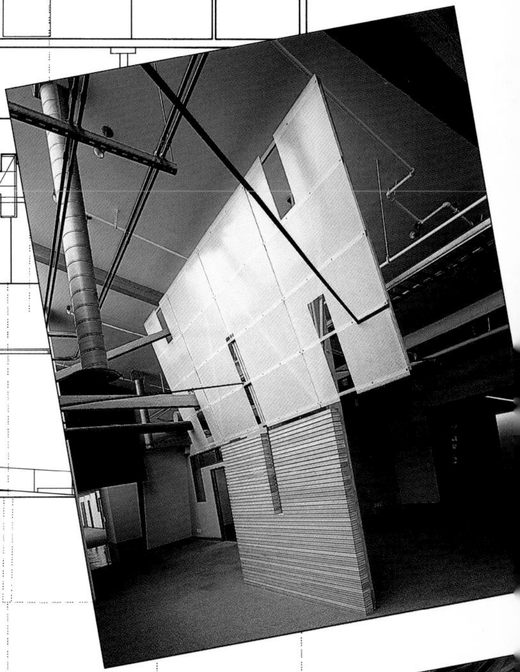

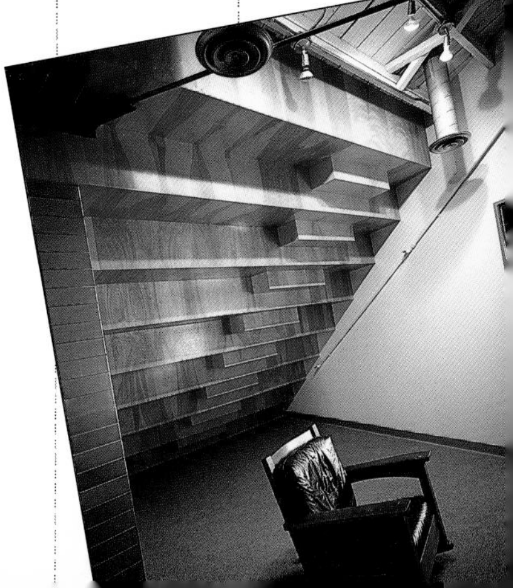

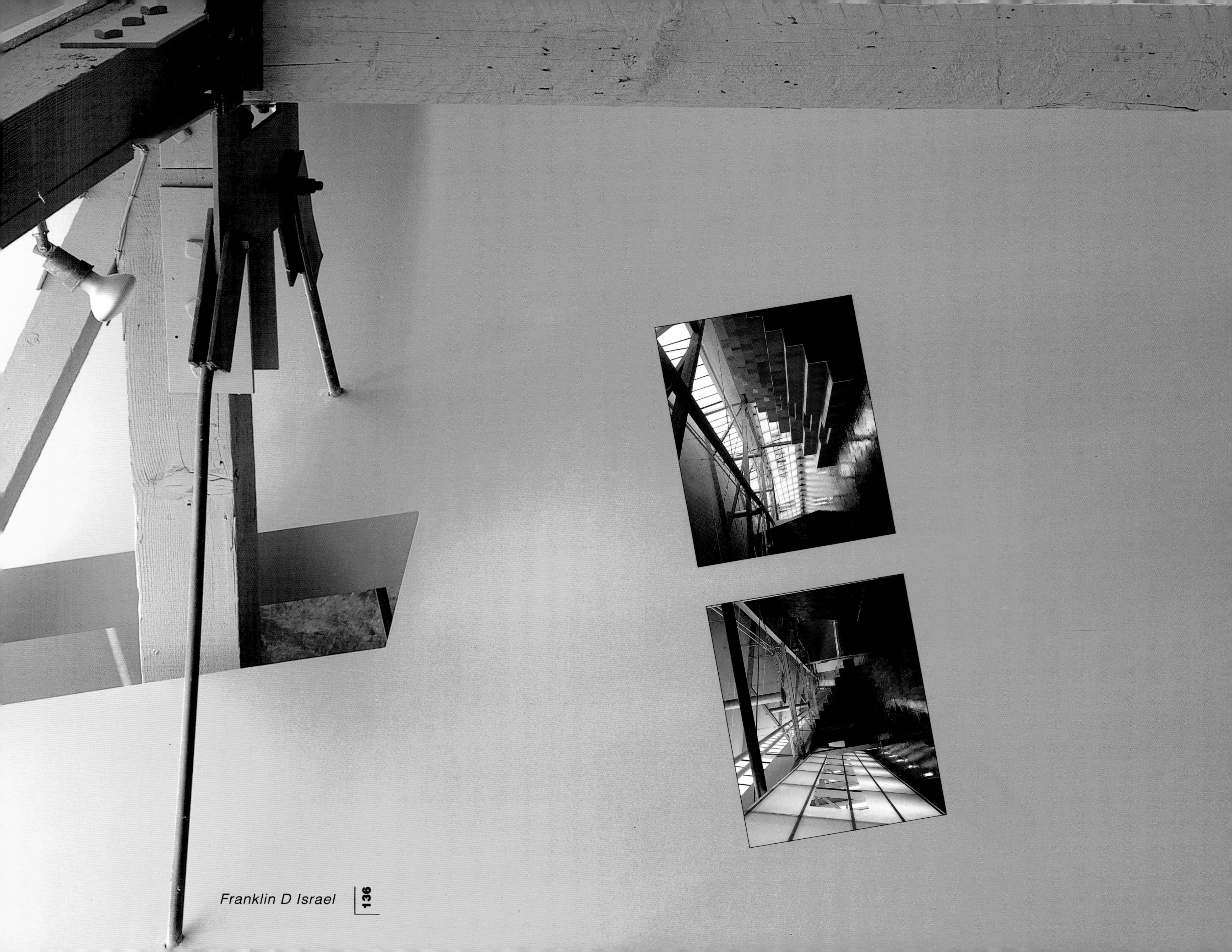

S TRICK HOUSE

1993

A master bedroom was placed on top of an existing house in the Hollywood Hills. The Stricks met on a street corner in New York ten years ago and their first home was a loft downtown. Since moving to Hollywood to write screenplays and sell used furniture, they have dreamed of an open plan bedroom space that would offer the freedom and dynamism they experienced while living in Manhattan. Their new room at the top, a single volume of space measuring 20 feet by 30 feet, contains sleeping, dressing, and bathing facilities. It opens onto a terrace with dramatic views of Hollywood and downtown LA. The facade dividing the inside from the outside is a floating wall suspended on counterweighted cables. A spa tub set into the facade offers the opportunity to appreciate the views in aquatic repose.

Hollywood, California

BELOW: Axonometric; P140: Longitudinal section with details of plan; P141: Floor plan.

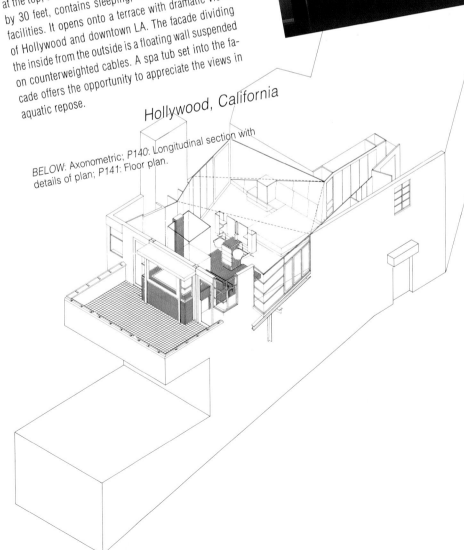

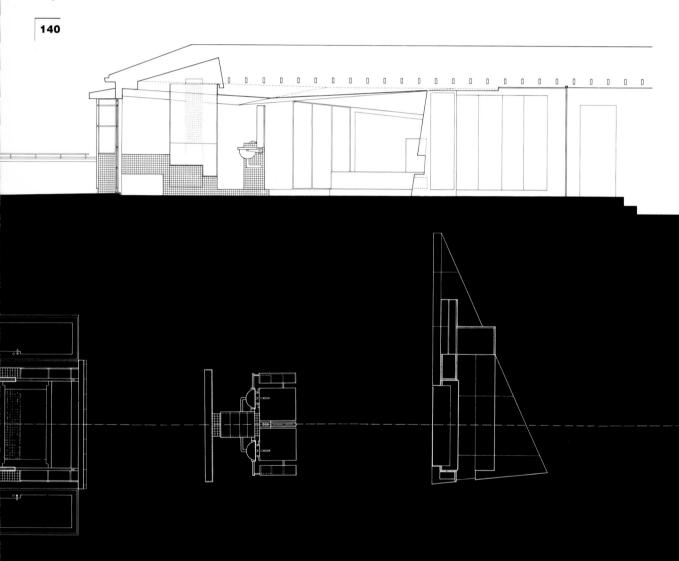

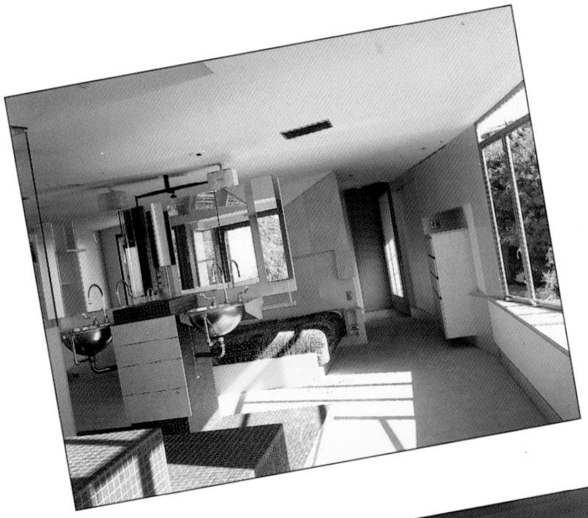

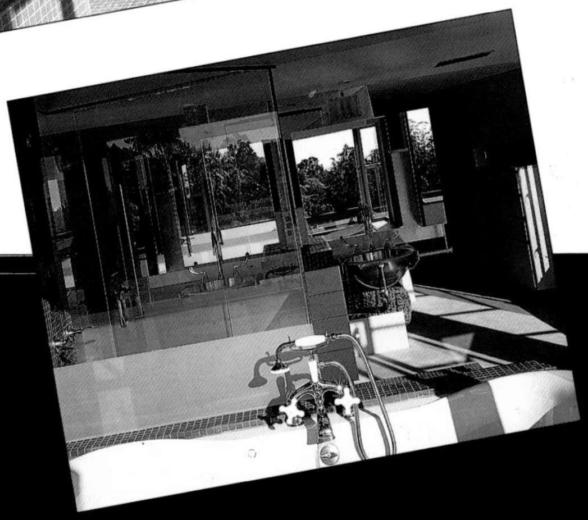

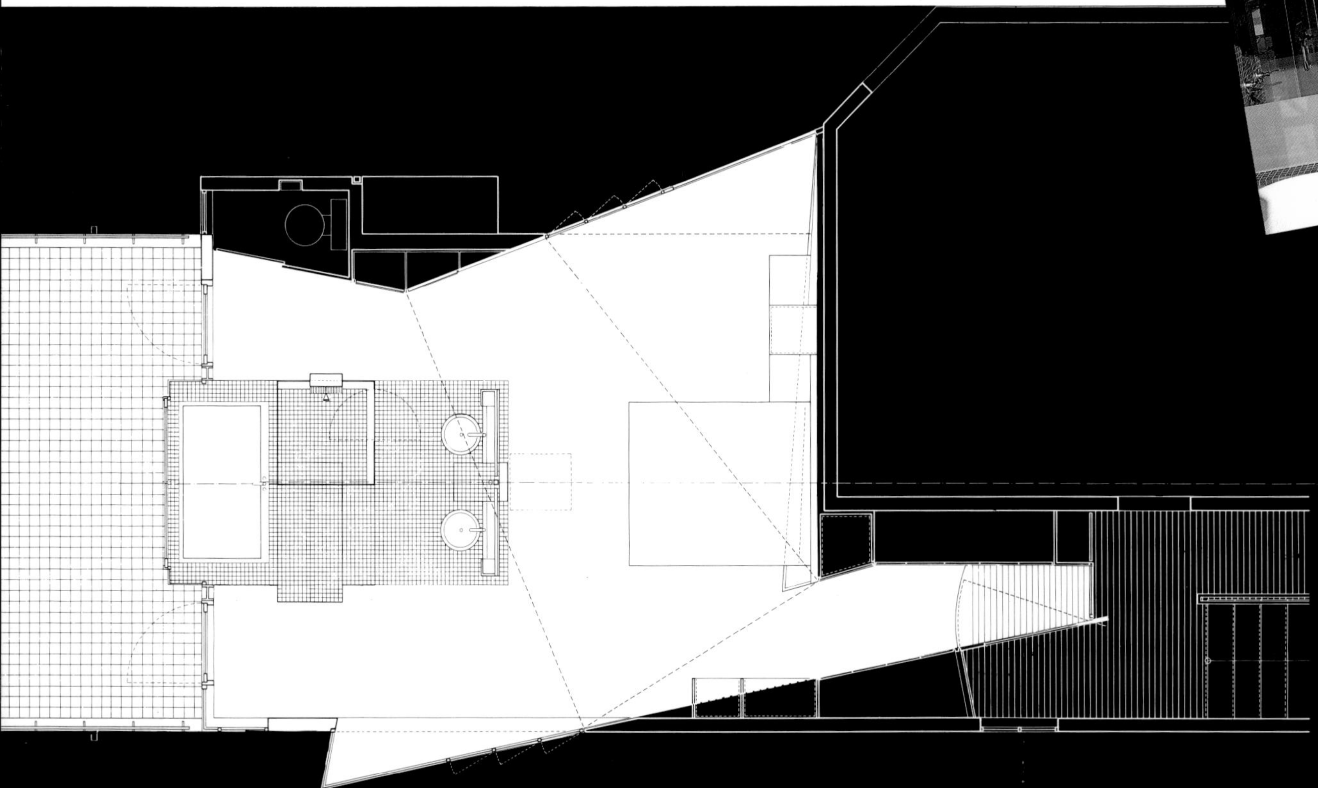

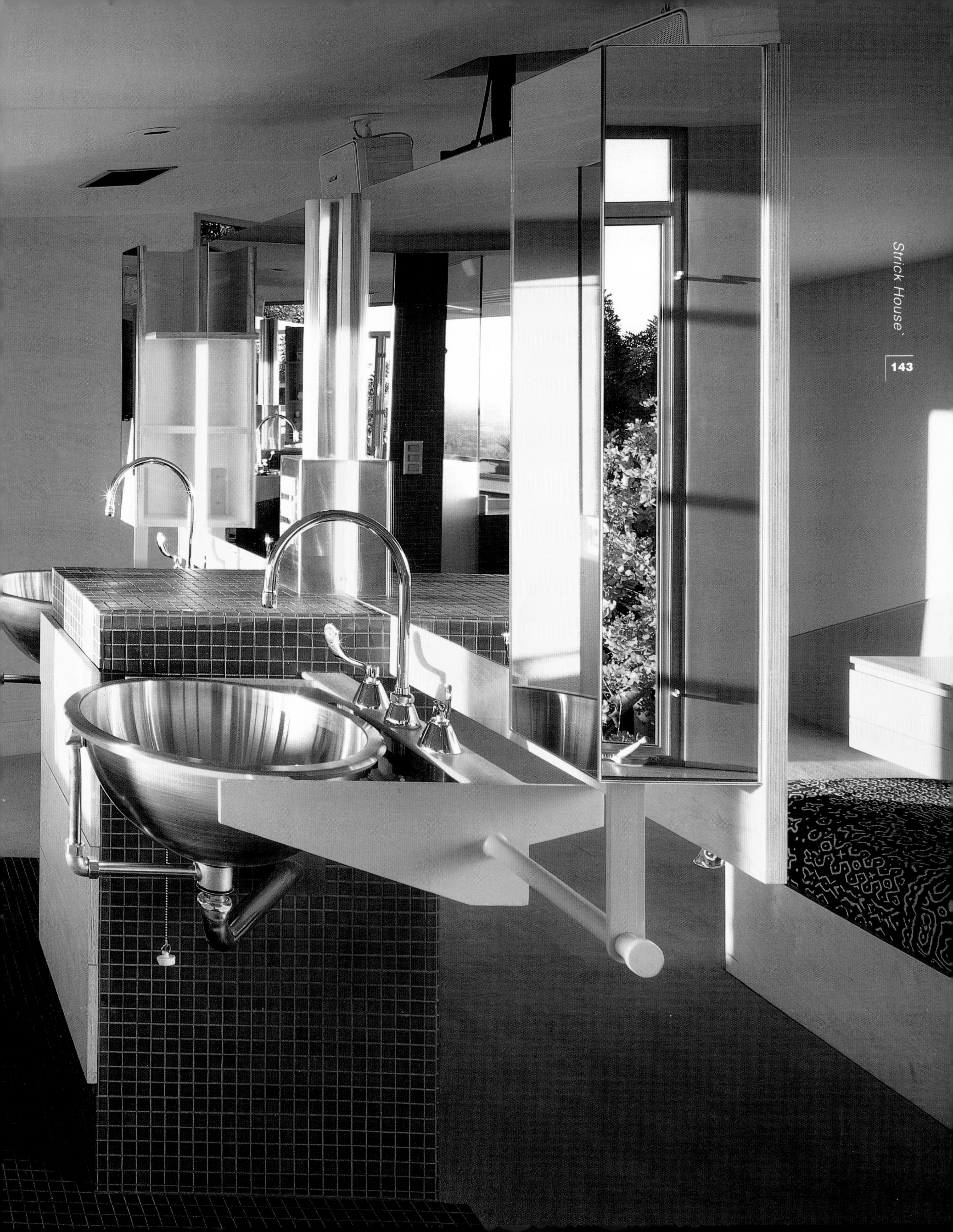

IOGRAPHY

Franklin D Israel was born in New York City in 1945. He received his education at Penn, Yale and Columbia, and was awarded the Rome Prize in Architecture in 1973. Currently, he is an Associate Professor in the School of Architecture and Urban Planning at the University of California, Los Angeles. He was a Visiting Professor at the Graduate School of Design of Harvard University in 1989-90, and has lectured at Columbia, Harvard, Berkeley, and numerous institutions in America and abroad.

The firm of Franklin D Israel Design Associates was founded in 1983. Before that time, Israel was with Giovanni Pasanella in New York and Llewelyn-Davies, Weeks, Forestier-Walker and Bor in London and Tehran. He was also involved in several small design partnerships working on projects in New York and Los Angeles. From 1978 to 1979 he served as an art director at Paramount Pictures.

Among the recent works produced by the firm are the offices for Limelight Productions, Hollywood, Bright and Associates, Venice, and Virgin Records, Beverly Hills. Residential work includes a Malibu beach house for Mr and Mrs Robert Altman and Los Angeles home of artist Richard Newton and designer Michele Lamy. Articles on Israel's work have appeared in journals such as *Lotus, Architectural Digest, Architectural Review, Progressive Architecture, Architectural Record, The New York Times* and his work was featured in the recent *World Cities: Los Angeles* published by Academy Editions.

In the autumn of 1989 Israel mounted an exhibition at the Walker Art Center entitled 'Six Mementos for the Next Millennium', the first in the series 'Architecture Tomorrow'. The show travelled to San Francisco's Museum of Modern Art and then to the Murray Feldman Gallery at the Pacific Design Center in Los Angeles.